THIS IS A BOOK ABOUT STREET FOOD

THIS IS
A BOOK
ABOUT
STREET
FOOD

BRENDAN PANG

Author of *This Is a Book About Noodles* and
This Is a Book About Dumplings

PAGE STREET
PUBLISHING CO.

PAGE STREET
PUBLISHING CO.

Distributed by Macmillan, sales in Canada by The Canadian Manda Group.

28 27 26 25 24   1 2 3 4 5

ISBN-13: 979-8-89003-024-5

Library of Congress Control Number: 2023944949

Edited by Marissa Giambelluca
Design by Page Street Publishing Co.
Photography by Wei Kang Liao
Illustrations by Nikki Singh

Printed and bound in China

THIS BOOK IS DEDICATED TO MY GRANDMÈRE, JOSEPHINE KON-YU.
SINCE MY EARLIEST DAYS, YOU'VE BEEN MY CULINARY COMPASS,
GUIDING ME THROUGH THE KITCHEN AND TEACHING ME THE ART OF
SAVORING GOOD FOOD. YOU INSTILLED IN ME A PROFOUND APPRECIATION
FOR OUR MAURITIAN CULTURE, SHOWING ME HOW THE SIMPLE ACT OF
COOKING CAN BE A POWERFUL FORM OF CONNECTION AND SHARING. YOUR
INFLUENCE IS THE SECRET INGREDIENT IN EVERY DISH I CREATE,
AND YOU CONTINUE TO BE MY GREATEST KITCHEN MUSE. THANK YOU,
GRANDMÈRE, FOR BEING MY ULTIMATE INSPIRATION—BOTH IN
AND OUTSIDE THE KITCHEN.

CONTENTS

INTRODUCTION

Hey there, food lovers! Welcome to my passion project—a cookbook that's going to take you on a whirlwind culinary tour of Asian street food. Here, you'll find recipes for ready-to-eat food you would normally buy from vendors on the street or in open-air markets—food that's often cheap, local and packed with flavor but made in the comfort of your own kitchen. If you've ever dreamed of wandering through bustling markets in Asia, sampling delectable bites from various stalls, then you're in for a treat.

While writing this book, I wanted to be based in Asia, specifically the bustling street food hub that is Taipei, to make this experience as authentic as possible for you. Teaming up with local creatives and soaking up Taipei's boundless creative energy has been a dream come true, and I can't wait to share that with you.

Influenced by my travels, this cookbook's got it all—from iconic dishes like Hong Kong fried noodles to Taiwanese oyster omelet and finger-licking snacks like Vietnamese rice paper rolls, Mauritian samosas and Malaysian *roti canai*. Each chapter is like a stroll down the food stalls of Asia's most exciting cities, but with a fun twist that you can easily re-create at home.

Now, about those recipes! If you're a noodle fanatic, the Hong Kong–Style Fried Noodles (page 17) are a must-try. Imagine springy noodles stir-fried with a medley of savory pork and a medley of veggies, all coated in a luscious sauce. For seafood lovers, the Fried Oyster Omelet (page 59) offers a rich blend of fresh oysters swaddled in a crispy yet gooey egg blanket—a real texture explosion.

But let's not forget the snacks. Craving something light and fresh? Fresh Prawn Rice Paper Rolls (page 111) are your portable salad meets finger food, perfect for a light lunch or a picnic. In the mood for some flaky, doughy goodness? Potato and Beef Samosa (page 103) and Roti Canai with Butter Bean Curry (page 115) are your go-tos—a fusion of spices and textures wrapped in crispy perfection.

And for dessert? Say hello to Soy Milk Pudding (Douhua) (page 142)—a silky, light-as-air sweet treat that proves tofu isn't just for savory dishes. With the perfect hint of sweetness, it's the ultimate palate cleanser.

What makes this cookbook truly special is that each recipe comes with my personal tips and kitchen hacks. Whether you're a novice or a seasoned chef, I've got you covered, making these dishes super approachable. So grab your apron, because you're about to teleport your taste buds to street corners from Tokyo to Mumbai with 60 of my favorite recipes, all without leaving your kitchen. Ready for this delicious journey? Let's go!

ONE

DUMPLINGS, NOODLES & RICE

It's not unintentional that this chapter starts where I left off with my first two cookbooks, *This Is a Book About Dumplings* and *This Is a Book About Noodles*. Dumplings, noodles and rice are not only foods that everyone loves, but more importantly, they are the culinary backbone of bustling markets and street food stalls across Asia.

Dumplings, those pockets of joy filled with a burst of flavor, represent the essence of handcrafted comfort. From the dimly lit stalls of Hong Kong to the busy lanes of Taipei, each dumpling carries with it generations of culinary wisdom and cultural heritage.

Noodles, the epitome of slurpable satisfaction, are the street food superstar. Whether tangled in a savory stir-fry like Hong-Kong–Style Fried Noodles (page 17) or swimming in a spice-driven broth like Taiwanese Beef Noodles (page 21), noodles offer endless possibilities for texture and taste.

Rice, the eternal companion of every Asian meal, serves as a canvas for culinary creativity. Be it the fluffy jasmine rice in the Fried Rice with BBQ Pork and Prawns (page 26) or the fragrant basmati in my Indian Fragrant Lamb Biryani (page 31), rice is more than just a side—it's a stage where spices, meats and vegetables come together in a harmonious dance.

In this chapter, I'm going to show you how to make these classics from scratch, and I'll share some cool tips and tricks along the way. You'll learn not just how to cook them but also why they're made the way they are.

So, let's get started. Pick up your cooking utensils and get ready for a tasty adventure with dumplings, rice and noodles. Trust me—it's a journey worth savoring every bite!

PORK AND CABBAGE DUMPLINGS (JIAOZI)

Jiaozi is a type of dumpling commonly eaten throughout most parts of China. As well as serving its purpose as a modest meal, it is considered a symbol of good fortune, resembling the shape of an ancient Chinese gold ingot. Street vendors serve jiaozi in so many ways, from steamed to panfried, and with a variety of fillings. This recipe is one of the most popular variations, and rightly so! The combination of the fresh cabbage cutting through the savoriness of the pork is not only a delicious pairing but also considered clean- and fresh-tasting, which is why it is eaten so commonly and at any time of the day.

MAKES 36 DUMPLINGS

Pork and Cabbage Filling

5.3 oz (150 g) napa cabbage, shredded finely

¼ tsp salt

12.3 oz (350 g) fatty ground pork

2 spring onions, chopped finely

4 tbsp (20 g) finely grated fresh ginger

2 tbsp (30 ml) light soy sauce

1 tbsp (15 ml) Shaoxing rice wine

1 tbsp (15 ml) sesame oil

Pinch of ground white pepper

1 tsp cornstarch, plus more for dusting

36 round dumpling wrappers

Dumpling Dipping Sauce

2 tbsp (30 ml) light soy sauce

2 tbsp (30 ml) Chinese black vinegar

1 tsp sesame oil

1 tbsp (15 ml) Chinese chili oil

Make the filling: Place the shredded cabbage in a colander that has been set over a large bowl, add the salt and mix well. Set aside for 15 minutes. Then, using your hands, squeeze firmly to extract all the liquid. Transfer the cabbage to a separate large bowl, add the pork, spring onions, ginger, light soy sauce, wine, sesame oil, white pepper and cornstarch and mix vigorously in one direction until the mixture binds. Cover and let rest in the fridge for 30 minutes.

Dust a baking sheet with cornstarch. Working with one dumpling wrapper at a time, place 1 heaping teaspoon of filling in the center. Shape the wrapper around the filling to form a taco shape. Use your thumb, index and middle fingers to make a W shape at one end of the folded dumpling and press together to seal. Pinch the folded dumpling skin together until you reach the halfway point of the seam. Transfer to the prepared baking sheet and cover loosely with a clean, damp tea towel. Repeat the process to form the remaining dumplings.

Make the dumpling dipping sauce: In a small serving bowl, stir together the light soy sauce, black vinegar, sesame oil and chili oil until well combined. Set aside.

Cook the dumplings in a large pot of boiling water until cooked through, 4 to 6 minutes. Remove from the water, using a slotted spoon, and transfer to a serving dish. Serve with the dumpling dipping sauce.

NOTES

- White cabbage can be substituted here for napa cabbage but should be sautéed or blanched first to help soften it.
- Chinese chili oil can be found at most Asian supermarkets.

EGG-SKIN PRAWN DUMPLINGS

I first learned about egg-skin dumplings (*dan jiao*) in a small hole-in-the-wall hot pot restaurant down a random alleyway in Taiwan, China. I was intrigued because I've only ever eaten dumplings with pastry made of wheat flour, so I immediately felt that it was something I wanted to re-create. These morsels are made with an omelet-style wrapper instead, and once formed to contain the filling, they are then cooked in a broth or, as in my recipe, with a glossy, savory gravy sauce. Yes, these may seem a little labor-intensive, but once you get into the rhythm of forming these dumplings, you won't want to stop. They are fun to make and, more importantly, so delicious!

MAKES 12 DUMPLINGS

Prawn Filling

7 oz (200 g) prawns, chopped

¼ cup (12 g) chopped garlic chives

½ tsp grated fresh ginger

1 tsp light soy sauce

1 tsp Shaoxing rice wine

½ tsp sesame oil

1 tsp cornstarch

Pinch of salt

Pinch of ground white pepper

Egg Skin

4 large eggs

1 tbsp (8 g) cornstarch

2 tsp (10 ml) water

Vegetable oil spray

Gravy

2 cups + 2 tbsp (500 ml) chicken stock

1 tbsp (15 ml) light soy sauce

1 tbsp (15 ml) oyster sauce

1 tbsp (15 ml) Shaoxing rice wine

1 tsp sugar

Cornstarch slurry (1 tsp cornstarch mixed with 2 tsp [10 ml] water)

Chopped fresh chives, for serving

Make the filling: In a medium-sized bowl, combine the prawns, garlic chives, ginger, light soy sauce, wine, sesame oil, cornstarch and a pinch each of salt and white pepper. Mix vigorously in one direction until the mixture binds. Cover and let rest in the fridge for 30 minutes.

Make the egg skin: In a small bowl, whisk together the eggs, cornstarch and water. Heat a nonstick skillet over medium heat and lightly spray with vegetable oil spray. Lower the heat and spoon about 2 tablespoons (30 ml) of the egg mixture into the pan, spreading with the back of the spoon to form a 4-inch (10-cm) circle.

When the bottom is cooked but the top is still a little wet, spoon 1 heaping teaspoon of the filling onto the middle of the egg skin, then fold the egg skin over to form a semicircle. Gently press the edges to seal. Remove from the pan and set aside. Repeat until all the dumplings have been formed.

Make the gravy: In a medium-sized saucepan, combine the chicken stock, light soy sauce, oyster sauce, wine and sugar over medium heat. Bring to a boil, then add the egg dumplings. Lower the heat and simmer for 6 to 8 minutes, or until the filling in the dumplings is cooked through. Transfer the dumplings to your serving dish. Thicken the sauce by whisking in the cornstarch slurry, until a gravy consistency is formed. Pour over the dumplings and sprinkle with chopped chives. Serve immediately.

NOTE

- To make this recipe pescatarian, substitute vegetable or seafood stock for the chicken stock.

HONG KONG–STYLE FRIED NOODLES

Say hello to the ultimate fast-food delight that's a staple in the buzzing streets of Hong Kong and a star on dim sum tables worldwide. This dish brings together the smoky, wok-charred flavor of stir-fried noodles with a medley of fresh veggies and your choice of protein—I'm using pork shoulder for its tenderness and rich, savory flavor. This recipe is quick and scrumptious and embodies the very spirit of Hong Kong's vibrant street food culture. Whether you're new to the art of wok cooking or a seasoned pro, this offers a one-way ticket to an authentic culinary adventure. So grab your chopsticks and let's get frying!

SERVES 2

- -

Pork Marinade

7 oz (200 g) pork shoulder, sliced into thin strips

1 tbsp (15 ml) Shaoxing rice wine

2 tsp (5 g) cornstarch

¼ tsp salt

Stir-Fry

8 oz (225 g) fresh thin egg noodles

4 tbsp (60 ml) vegetable oil, divided

½ onion, sliced thinly

½ carrot, cut into matchsticks

1 tsp minced fresh ginger

1 tsp minced garlic

2 tbsp (30 ml) oyster sauce

1 tbsp (15 ml) light soy sauce

1 tsp sugar

½ tsp ground white pepper

1 bunch kailan (Chinese broccoli), washed and trimmed

Marinate the pork: In a medium-sized bowl, combine the pork strips, wine, cornstarch and salt, and mix well. Set aside, covered, for 20 minutes.

Begin the stir-fry: Bring a pot of water to a boil and cook the noodles for 2 to 3 minutes, or until just cooked through. Drain, then set aside.

Place a wok over high heat and add 2 tablespoons (30 ml) vegetable oil. When hot, add the marinated pork and stir-fry until browned, about 5 minutes. Remove the pork from the wok and set aside. Add another 2 tablespoons (30 ml) of vegetable oil to the wok. When hot, add the onion, carrot, ginger and garlic. Stir-fry for 2 to 3 minutes, then add the drained noodles. Add the oyster sauce, light soy sauce, sugar, white pepper and *kailan*, and toss, cooking for an additional 2 to 3 minutes. Add the cooked pork back to the wok, toss and serve.

SILKY EGG AND PRAWN HOR FUN NOODLES

Hor fun noodles are wide, flat rice noodles commonly used in Chinese and Southeast Asian cuisines. They're usually made from rice flour and water, resulting in a silky, chewy texture that's perfect for soaking up flavor. In this recipe, the velvety noodles are tossed with succulent prawns and fluffy scrambled eggs. It's a flavor-packed experience you'd find in the bustling hawker centers (open-air food courts) and street food stalls of Southeast Asia. Quick to whip up but long-lasting in memory, this is the ideal recipe for when you're craving something that's both familiar and adventurous.

SERVES 2

- -

Stir-Fry

15 oz (420 g) fresh wide rice noodles (hor fun)

4 tbsp (60 ml) vegetable oil, divided

2 tbsp (30 ml) light soy sauce

5 cloves garlic, sliced thinly

4 tsp (20 g) thinly sliced fresh ginger

2 spring onions, chopped

12 large prawns, peeled and deveined

3 choy sum (Chinese flowering cabbage) stalks, sliced thinly lengthwise

5 fresh shiitake mushrooms, sliced thinly

Hor Fun Gravy

4¼ cups (1 L) chicken stock

2 tbsp (30 ml) oyster sauce

1 tbsp (15 ml) light soy sauce

1 tbsp (15 ml) Shaoxing rice wine

1 tsp sesame oil

1 tsp sugar

½ tsp ground white pepper

Cornstarch slurry (3 tbsp [24 g] cornstarch mixed with 5 tbsp [75 ml] water)

2 large eggs, beaten lightly

Start the stir-fry: To separate the fresh noodles, rinse under water to remove the oily residue. Place in a bowl of warm water and gently separate with your hands. Drain and set aside.

Place a wok or large skillet over high heat and add 2 tablespoons (30 ml) of vegetable oil. Spread the noodles over the surface area of the wok and let fry for 1 to 2 minutes. Add the light soy sauce and toss to coat, cooking for an additional 1 to 2 minutes. Transfer the cooked noodles to a bowl and set aside.

Place the wok back over high heat and add another 2 tablespoons (30 ml) of vegetable oil. When hot, add the garlic, ginger and spring onions, and stir-fry for 20 seconds, or until fragrant. Add the prawns and stir-fry until just cooked through, about 2 minutes. Add the *choy sum* and shiitake mushrooms, and stir-fry for about 1 minute.

Make the gravy: Add the chicken stock, oyster sauce, light soy sauce, wine, sesame oil, sugar and white pepper to the wok. Lower the heat to a simmer and stir while pouring in the cornstarch slurry, to thicken to a gravylike consistency. While simmering, gently stir in the beaten eggs to form silky ribbons. Taste and adjust the seasoning as desired.

Plate up your fried rice noodles and generously ladle the steaming-hot gravy over them. Serve immediately.

TAIWANESE BEEF NOODLES

This culinary gem is a cornerstone of Taiwanese street food and a global favorite for its rich, complex flavors. If you are yet to try it, imagine slow-cooked beef in a deeply aromatic broth, coupled with springy noodles and a sprinkle of fresh greens. The combination of spice, savory notes and heartwarming broth makes this more than just a meal—it's an experience.

SERVES 4

Broth

1¾ lb (800 g) boneless beef shank

2 tbsp (30 ml) vegetable oil

1 medium-sized onion, sliced

3 spring onions, cut into 2" (5-cm) lengths

4 slices fresh ginger

6 cloves garlic, sliced

3 tbsp (39 g) spicy bean paste

½ cup (120 ml) light soy sauce

½ cup (120 ml) dark soy sauce

½ cup (120 ml) Shaoxing rice wine

2 tomatoes, quartered

1 tbsp (13 g) sugar

1 tsp ground white pepper

1 tsp salt

8½ cups (2 L) water

Spice Sachet

4 star anise pods

2 cinnamon sticks

2 bay leaves

1 tbsp (5 g) whole Sichuan peppercorns (optional)

1 dried orange peel (optional)

For Serving

2 bundles flour noodles

2 cups (200 g) bok choy

Sliced spring onion

Chopped fresh cilantro

Make the broth: Fill a large pot with water and add the beef shank. Bring to a boil and cook over high heat for 5 to 10 minutes, or until just cooked through. Remove the cooked beef from the pot, rinse under cold water and slice into ⅜-inch (1-cm)-thick slices. Discard the cooking liquid.

In a wok or large skillet over medium-high heat, heat 2 tablespoons (30 ml) of vegetable oil. When hot, add the onion, spring onions, ginger and garlic, and stir-fry until the onion starts to become translucent. Add the sliced beef and spicy bean paste, and stir-fry for an additional 2 to 3 minutes. Add the light soy sauce, dark soy sauce, wine, tomatoes, sugar, white pepper and salt, and stir-fry for 10 minutes, or until the tomatoes have softened. Transfer to a pot over high heat and add 8½ cups (2 L) of water. Bring to a boil.

Meanwhile, make the spice sachet: In a small piece of cheesecloth, combine the star anise pods, cinnamon sticks, bay leaves, Sichuan peppercorns (if using) and orange peel (if using), and tie with kitchen twine to enclose. Add the spice sachet to the broth and lower the heat to low. Simmer for 1 to 1½ hours, or until the meat is tender, then remove the spice sachet and turn off the heat.

When ready to serve, bring a medium-sized pot of water to a boil over high heat and cook the noodles for 2 to 3 minutes, or until just cooked through. Drain and divide among your serving bowls. Cook the bok choy in the same boiling water as the noodles for 1 minute, then drain and divide among your serving bowls. Into each bowl, ladle a generous amount of soup along with some beef shank. Garnish with spring onion and cilantro.

INSTANT POT® MUSHROOM CONGEE

While congee has its roots deep in Asian cuisine, from the bustling street food scenes of Hong Kong to the family tables of mainland China, my version elevates the classic by infusing it with the rich, earthy flavors of mushrooms. And the best part? Your Instant Pot does all the heavy lifting. In less time than it takes to order takeout, you will be able to cook up a pot of delicious soul-warming congee. Read on to find out how easy it is to make this crowd-pleaser.

SERVES 2 TO 3

- -

Congee

1 scant cup (180 g) uncooked jasmine rice

7⅓ cups (1.75 L) vegetable stock, plus more if needed

1 tsp salt

2.1 oz (60 g) dried sliced shiitake mushrooms, rinsed

3 cloves garlic, sliced thinly

1 oz (30 g) fresh ginger, julienned

For Serving

Light soy sauce

Chili oil (optional)

Finely chopped spring onion

Fried garlic flakes

Toasted white sesame seeds

Make the congee: Place the rice in a strainer and rinse under running water for 30 seconds, making sure to rub the grains with your fingers to remove some starch. Drain, then transfer to the insert of an Instant Pot along with the vegetable stock, salt, shiitake mushrooms, garlic and ginger. Close the Instant Pot, lock and set on high pressure for 30 minutes.

Once finished cooking, let the pressure release naturally, then open the lid and stir. The consistency should be like porridge. You may add more stock to thin it out slightly, keeping in mind that the rice will thicken as it cools. To serve, drizzle with light soy sauce and chili oil (if using), then top with spring onion, fried garlic flakes and toasted white sesame seeds. Serve immediately.

NOTE

- To make this on the stovetop, in a large pot with a lid, combine the rice, stock, salt, shiitake mushrooms, garlic and ginger, cover and place over high heat. Bring to a boil and simmer, stirring, for 1½ hours, or until cooked and a porridgelike consistency is achieved.

TAIWANESE STICKY RICE ROLLS (FAN TUAN)

Fan tuan is a sticky rice roll that originated in eastern China but is now a classic breakfast item around Shanghai and Taiwan. My first taste of fan tuan was at a small corner street stall in Taipei and was one of those mind-blowing food experiences that checked all the boxes. It's salty, a little sour, crunchy and soft, and can be customized to your very own taste. The sticky rice sits in a wooden basket, steaming hot and ready to go, and a whole variety of fillings are on offer, but the usual suspects include a crunchy Chinese donut, some preserved Asian greens (or kimchi, in my recipe) and meat floss (dried meat that has been shredded to a cotton candy–like consistency) of some sort. Whether you're trying it for breakfast or not, have some fun and get creative trying this delicious rice roll out!

MAKES 4 ROLLS

- -

Rounded 2 cups (375 g) uncooked glutinous rice

1 youtiao (Chinese donut stick)

4 large eggs

1 cup (100 g) meat floss

1 cup + 2½ tsp (262 g) chopped kimchi

2 spring onions, chopped

Toasted white sesame seeds

To steam the glutinous rice, rinse through a strainer until the water becomes clear. Place in a bowl and cover with water. Let soak overnight or for at least 6 hours. Drain well, then transfer to a cheesecloth-lined steamer basket. Fold in the corners of the cheesecloth to cover the rice completely and cover the steamer with a lid. Bring the water to a full boil over medium-high heat and steam for about 30 minutes, or until tender. Keep the rice covered in the steamer until you're ready to assemble.

Toast the *youtiao* in a 400°F (200°C) oven for 6 to 8 minutes, or until crisp, then divide into four pieces. Fry the eggs to your liking. A well-cooked egg is easier to work with when assembling.

To assemble the fan tuan, thinly spread ½ to 1 cup (100 to 200 g) of the cooked sticky rice on a piece of plastic wrap about 5 x 7 inches (12.5 x 18 cm) in size. Place one piece of youtiao in the center along with one-quarter of the meat floss, one-quarter of the kimchi, one fried egg, some chopped spring onions and a sprinkle of sesame seeds. Use the plastic wrap to roll and squeeze all the ingredients tightly into an oblong roll. If you have a bamboo sushi mat, this makes the wrapping process easier. Repeat this process until all four rolls are formed. Slice in half and serve immediately.

NOTE

- Youtiao can be found frozen at most Asian supermarkets. Fried wonton skins can be substituted if youtiao are unavailable. Meat floss can also be found at most Asian supermarkets.

FRIED RICE WITH BBQ PORK AND PRAWNS

Get ready to experience the ultimate trifecta of flavors. This dish is where smoky barbecued pork meets succulent prawns, all tossed with fluffy fried rice. It's more than just a meal; it's the king of quick eats. Whether you're cooking for a weeknight dinner or impressing guests, this fried rice dish offers a gourmet touch with everyday ease. Dive into the recipe and find out how you can whip up this culinary masterpiece in your own kitchen.

SERVES 6

- -

Rice Seasoning

Pinch of ground white pepper

½ tsp sugar

1 tbsp (15 ml) light soy sauce

1 tbsp (15 ml) Asian fish sauce

2 tbsp (30 ml) sambal oelek

2 tsp (10 ml) hot water

Fried Rice

5 tbsp (75 ml) vegetable oil, divided

2 large eggs, beaten

2 cloves garlic, minced

5.5 oz (150 g) raw prawn, chopped roughly

5.5 oz (150 g) char siu (Chinese barbecued pork), chopped

1 medium-sized onion, chopped

5¼ cups (887 g) leftover cooked white rice

1 cup (104 g) bean sprouts

2 spring onions, chopped

Make the rice seasoning: In a small bowl, combine the white pepper, sugar, light soy sauce, fish sauce, sambal oelek and hot water, and stir until well combined. Set aside.

Make the fried rice: Heat your wok over high heat and add 2 tablespoons (30 ml) of vegetable oil followed by the beaten eggs. Cook, scrambling with a spatula to break into smaller pieces, for 2 to 3 minutes. Once cooked, transfer the scrambled eggs to a bowl and set aside. Return your wok to high heat and add another 2 tablespoons (30 ml) of vegetable oil followed by the garlic. Stir-fry until fragrant, about 1 minute, then add the prawns and stir-fry for an additional 2 minutes, or until just cooked through. Transfer to a bowl and set aside.

Return your wok to high heat and add 1 tablespoon (15 ml) of vegetable oil, followed by the *char siu*. Stir-fry for 20 seconds, lower the heat slightly, then add the onion. Stir-fry until translucent, about 2 minutes. Increase the heat to high and add the cooked rice. Use your spatula to flatten the rice and break up any clumps. Once the rice is warmed, evenly pour the rice seasoning over the rice and toss until well coated. Add the scrambled egg, prawns, bean sprouts and spring onions, and toss for an additional minute until well combined. Taste and adjust the seasoning as desired. Serve immediately.

NOTE

- Char siu can be found at most Chinese takeout shops. It is quite a lengthy process to make at home, so I recommend purchasing some when you're out. If you can't find any, *lap cheong* (Chinese sausage) is a great alternative and can be found at most Asian supermarkets.

HAINANESE CHICKEN RICE

If I had to pick one death row meal, this would be it. Chicken rice transcends its humble ingredients to offer a global passport of flavors. With its origins in Hainanese cuisine, this Singaporean version has become an iconic comfort food that graces hawker stalls, family tables and even gourmet restaurants. Imagine succulent chicken paired with fragrant rice, all brought to life with zesty sauces and garnishes. It's a simple dish, yet every bite is a burst of complex tastes and textures. Whether you're a first-timer or a chicken rice pro, this recipe is your ticket to a culinary journey you won't forget!

SERVES 4

Chicken

1 (scant 3½-lb [1.5-kg]) chicken

14¾ cups (3.5 L) water

4 or 5 slices fresh ginger

2 spring onions

1½ tsp (9 g) salt

Rice

Fat from chicken's back cavity

4 cloves garlic, chopped finely

1 shallot, chopped finely

3 cups + 1½ tbsp (610 g) uncooked jasmine rice, washed

3⅔ cups (875 ml) reserved chicken poaching broth

2 tsp (12 g) salt

Chili Sauce

1 tbsp (15 ml) fresh lime juice

2 tbsp (30 ml) reserved chicken poaching broth

2 tsp (8 g) sugar

4 tbsp (60 ml) Sriracha

4 cloves garlic, grated finely

1 (1" [2.5-cm])-long piece fresh ginger, grated finely

Cook the chicken: Trim off all the fat from the back cavity, setting it aside for the rice. Place a large pot over high heat and add the water, sliced ginger, spring onions and salt. Bring to a boil, then carefully lower the chicken into the water, breast side up. Bring to a boil again, then lower the heat to a simmer and let cook, partially covered, for 30 minutes. Turn off the heat and cover completely with the lid. Let sit for an additional 30 minutes. The residual heat will gently finish cooking the chicken. Remove the chicken, transfer it to an ice bath and let sit for 10 minutes to stop the cooking. Scoop out the ginger and spring onions, and reserve the remaining broth.

Cook the rice: In a medium-sized skillet over low to medium heat, heat the reserved chicken fat. Cook until the fat has rendered, then add the garlic and shallot. Cook, stirring, until fragrant, about 1 minute, then add the jasmine rice. Cook, stirring, for about 2 minutes, then transfer to a rice cooker and add the reserved chicken poaching broth and the salt. Turn on and let cook.

Make the chili sauce: In a small bowl, combine the lime juice, chicken poaching broth, sugar, Sriracha and grated garlic and ginger, and mix well. Set aside.

(continued)

HAINANESE CHICKEN RICE (CONTINUED)

2 spring onions, chopped finely

1 (1" [2.5-cm])-long piece fresh ginger, grated finely

⅓ cup + 4 tsp (100 ml) grapeseed oil

2 tsp (12 g) salt

1 tbsp (15 ml) sesame oil

Sliced cucumber

Fresh cilantro

Make the ginger and spring onion sauce: In a heatproof bowl, combine the spring onions and grated ginger. In a small pan, heat the grapeseed oil until just smoking, then pour that over the spring onions and ginger to sizzle. Add the salt and sesame oil, and mix well. Set aside.

To serve, carve the chicken as desired and plate with the cooked chicken rice and some slices of cucumber. Drizzle with the chili sauce and the ginger and spring onion sauce and top with fresh cilantro. Any remaining chicken poaching broth can be served on the side.

INDIAN FRAGRANT LAMB BIRYANI

Biryani is a one-pot wonder that is often found sizzling at street food stalls and family gatherings alike. In my Mauritian family, we would enjoy this meal (with beef) at most family occasions; however, on a recent trip to India, I stumbled upon a flavor-packed biryani with tender lamb and fragrant rice, and I had to make my own version for this book, bringing the vibrant energy of the street food scene right to your kitchen. Whether you're having a casual weeknight dinner or hosting a feast, this easy yet showstopping recipe is your go-to. Marinated lamb, aromatic spices and saffron-infused rice combine to create a dish that's both homey and exotic.

SERVES 6

Marinated Lamb

4½ lb (2 kg) boneless lamb shoulder or leg, cut into ¾" (2-cm) cubes

1¼ cups (300 ml) Greek yogurt

1 cup + 2 tsp (250 ml) water

¼ cup (60 ml) vegetable oil

2 tbsp (20 g) minced garlic

1 tbsp (5 g) minced fresh ginger

½ tsp ground turmeric

½ tsp ground cinnamon

1 tsp cayenne pepper

1 tsp ground cardamom

4 tsp (8 g) garam masala

4 tsp (8 g) ground coriander

2 tbsp (14 g) ground cumin

4 tbsp (28 g) paprika

2 tsp (12 g) salt

Fragrant Rice

2 tbsp (36 g) salt

10 cloves

5 dried bay leaves

1 star anise pod

6 green cardamom pods

2⅓ cups (450 g) uncooked basmati rice

Marinate the lamb: In a large bowl, combine the cubed lamb, yogurt, water, oil, garlic, ginger, turmeric, cinnamon, cayenne, cardamom, garam masala, coriander, cumin, paprika and salt, and toss well. Cover with plastic wrap and refrigerate for at least 1 hour, or ideally overnight.

Cook the fragrant rice: Fill a medium-sized pot with water, add the salt, cloves, bay leaves, star anise and cardamom pods, and bring to a boil. Add the rice, bring back to a boil, and cook for 4 to 5 minutes, or until just cooked through. The rice should still be firm, being as it will be cooked again afterward. Drain the rice and set it aside.

(continued)

INDIAN FRAGRANT LAMB BIRYANI (CONTINUED)

Biryani

½ cup (120 ml) ghee, divided

1 cup + 2 tsp (250 ml) water

½ cup (100 g) fried shallots

Salt

1 tsp saffron threads, soaked in 2 tbsp (30 ml) water

Chopped fresh cilantro, for serving

Cook the biryani: Place a large pot over medium heat and add ¼ cup (60 ml) of the ghee. Add the lamb, including any excess marinade, plus the water. Stir and bring to a boil, then lower the heat to low and simmer, covered, stirring occasionally, for 45 to 60 minutes, or until the lamb is tender.

Once cooked, top with the cooked rice and flatten with the back of a spatula. Scatter the fried shallots on top and drizzle the saffron and its soaking liquid over the rice, then add the remaining ¼ cup (60 ml) of ghee. Place the lid back on, turn the heat back to medium and, once steaming, lower the heat to low and cook for 25 to 30 minutes. Let rest for 10 minutes before serving, then garnish with cilantro.

NOTE

- Fried shallots can be found at most specialty and Asian supermarkets.

TWO

MEAT

Welcome to the mouthwatering chapter on meat dishes in the wondrous world of Asian street food. Whether it's sizzling on a grill, stewing in a pot or stir-fried to perfection, there's something undeniably comforting and satisfying about these dishes. This chapter is your VIP pass to some of the most unforgettable meaty experiences you can have without buying a plane ticket!

Ever walked through the night markets in Taipei? If so, you've probably come across Popcorn Chicken with Basil (page 38). This bad boy combines crispy bite-sized bits of fried chicken with aromatic basil leaves, creating a snack that's seriously addictive. It's the ultimate combo of textures and flavors that you'll learn to make right in your own kitchen.

I'll also venture to the bustling streets of Vietnam to master the art of their iconic Steamed Pork Buns (page 42). Soft, pillowy buns filled with flavorful pork and fun fillings like quail eggs—sounds like heaven, right? Don't worry; I've got you covered with tips to make them as authentic as the ones you'd find in Ho Chi Minh City.

And I can't forget the fiery and aromatic Spicy Thai Beef Basil (Pad Gra Pow) (page 49)! Imagine juicy beef tossed in a hot wok with spicy chiles and fragrant basil leaves. It's a dish that captures the essence of Thai cuisine and can ignite your taste buds with a single bite.

For all my meat-based recipes, I'll dive into the cooking techniques, key spices and stories that make these meaty marvels so special. You'll also find some killer tips to nail these dishes like a pro. So, heat up that wok—this chapter is going to be a roller coaster of delicious flavors and aromas!

FILIPINO DUMPLINGS (SIOMAI)

This popular street food gem has won hearts in the Philippines and beyond, and for good reason. If you haven't tried Filipino *siomai*, imagine tender pockets of ground pork and juicy prawn seasoned to perfection and wrapped in a delicate dumpling wrapper. Steamed until tender, these morsels are usually served with a side of soy sauce and calamansi (a cross between kumquat and wild mandarin orange) for that extra zing, but my favorite way to enjoy these is with fried garlic and a little kick of chile pepper.

SERVES 4

- -

Filling

3 dried shiitake mushrooms

10.5 oz (300 g) fatty ground pork

10.5 oz (300 g) raw prawn meat, chopped coarsely

½ carrot, grated

3 spring onions, chopped finely

Freshly ground black pepper

1 tbsp (15 ml) light soy sauce

1 tbsp (15 ml) oyster sauce

1 tbsp (15 ml) Shaoxing rice wine

1 tbsp (15 ml) sesame oil

1 tsp cornstarch

1 tsp sugar

1 tsp salt

Pinch of ground white pepper

Dumplings

35 large wonton wrappers

½ cup (65 g) finely chopped carrot

Fried Garlic and Soy

¼ cup (60 ml) vegetable oil

4 medium-sized cloves garlic, minced finely

½ cup (125 ml) soy sauce

1 long red chile pepper, sliced finely

1 tsp sesame oil

Make the filling: Soak the dried shiitake mushrooms in hot water until softened. Squeeze the excess water from the mushrooms, remove and discard the stems and chop finely. In a large bowl, combine the mushrooms with the pork, prawn meat, grated carrot, spring onions, black pepper, light soy sauce, oyster sauce, Shaoxing rice wine, sesame oil, cornstarch, sugar, salt and white pepper, and mix vigorously in one direction until the mixture binds. Cover the filling and let it rest in the fridge for 1 hour.

Form the dumplings: Make a circle with your thumb and index finger. Working with one wonton wrapper at a time, place one heaping teaspoon of filling in the center and nudge it down through the circle you've created with your hand. Gently squeeze into shape and pat down the filling with the back of a spoon. Gently tap the dumpling on your work surface so it can stand upright, then top with a small pinch of chopped carrot over the center. Repeat the process to form the remaining dumplings.

Line a bamboo steamer with parchment paper and place in a wok over high heat. Pour enough water into the wok to reach 1 inch (2.5 cm) below the bottom of the steamer. Once the water is boiling, steam the siomai in batches for 8 to 10 minutes, or until cooked through.

Make the fried garlic and soy: Heat the vegetable oil in a small skillet over medium-low heat. Add the garlic and cook until fragrant and golden, about 5 minutes, stirring if needed to prevent the edges from browning too much. Remove from the heat and transfer to a small bowl. Mix in the soy sauce, chile and sesame oil, and serve.

POPCORN CHICKEN WITH BASIL

Taiwanese fried chicken, in my opinion, is the ultimate street food delight! Whether you're strolling through the lanes of Taipei or re-creating this dish in your own kitchen, this is more than a meal—it's an event. Now, if you haven't tried it, imagine chunks of popcorn-sized chicken are marinated in a blend of spices and seasonings, coated with a crispy batter and deep-fried to golden perfection. But wait, there's more. A final dusting of a spice mixture with crispy fragrant basil leaves gives this chicken a kick that'll have you coming back for seconds—and maybe even thirds.

SERVES 4

Chicken

6 boneless chicken thighs, cut into 1¼" (3-cm) cubes

2½ tbsp (38 ml) light soy sauce

3 tbsp (45 ml) Shaoxing rice wine

1 tbsp (10 g) minced garlic

1 tbsp (6 g) Chinese five-spice powder

1 large egg

3½ tbsp (28 g) cornstarch

2 cups (256 g) tapioca starch

Vegetable oil

1 cup (40 g) fresh Thai basil leaves

Seasoning Mixture

1 tsp ground white pepper

1 tsp ground Sichuan pepper

2 tsp (12 g) salt

¼ tsp Chinese five-spice powder

Marinate the chicken: In a bowl, combine the chicken, light soy sauce, wine, minced garlic and five-spice powder. Set aside, covered, for 20 to 30 minutes. Then, stir in the egg and cornstarch until a wet batter forms around the chicken.

To fry, spread the tapioca starch in a baking dish and add the battered chicken pieces, tossing to coat. Let sit for 5 minutes to allow for the tapioca starch to stick.

Make the seasoning mixture: In a small bowl, stir together the white pepper, Sichuan pepper, salt and five-spice powder. Set aside.

To cook, fill a wok with vegetable oil about two-thirds of the way up. Heat to 350°F (180°C) over high heat and test by dipping a wooden chopstick into the oil; the chopstick will sizzle when the oil is ready. Deep-fry the basil leaves for 1 minute, or until crisp and translucent. Drain well and set aside. In the same oil, working in batches, deep-fry the chicken until golden brown, 3 to 4 minutes. Transfer to a baking sheet lined with paper towels, to drain. When all the chicken has been fried, fry all the pieces once more for 1 minute, or until super crisp, then drain again and season with the seasoning mixture.

BEEF SATAY WITH PEANUT SAUCE

Beef satay is a popular dish found in street food scenes from Indonesia to Malaysia and beyond. Think of it as tasty beef strips marinated in spices, skewered onto sticks and then grilled for a smoky finish. The best part? A yummy nutty sauce to dip it in. This dish is super flavorful and perfect for gatherings, quick snacks or even as a main course. Whether you're new to satay or already a fan, this recipe will make your grilling even better. So fire up that grill and get cooking!

SERVES 4

- -

Marinade

21 oz (600 g) rump steak, cut into roughly 1¼" (3-cm) cubes

1 clove garlic, grated finely

1 tbsp (7 g) ground cumin

1 tbsp (6 g) ground coriander

1 tsp ground turmeric

1 tbsp (15 ml) dark sweet soy sauce

1 tbsp (15 ml) vegetable oil

1 tsp sea salt

Satay Sauce

1 tbsp (15 ml) vegetable oil

1½ tbsp (23 g) Thai red curry paste

1 cup + 2 tsp (250 ml) coconut milk

2 tbsp (32 g) crunchy peanut butter

1 tsp Asian fish sauce

2 tsp (8 g) sugar

3 tbsp (36 g) crushed roasted peanuts

For Serving

Diced red onion

Diced cucumber

Fresh cilantro leaves

Marinate the beef: In a bowl, combine the cubed steak, garlic, cumin, coriander, turmeric, dark sweet soy sauce, oil and salt. Mix well and allow to rest for at least 10 minutes, or up to overnight in the fridge.

Soak 20 bamboo skewers in water for at least 30 minutes before you plan to cook the satay. Then, thread three or four pieces of the marinated meat onto each bamboo skewer. Discard the marinade.

Make the satay sauce: In a small saucepan, heat the vegetable oil over medium heat. Add the curry paste and cook for 1 minute, or until fragrant. Add the coconut milk, peanut butter, fish sauce and sugar. Stir in the crushed peanuts. Cook for an additional minute, then remove from the heat. Taste and adjust the seasoning with more fish sauce and/or sugar. Keep warm or reheat when ready to serve.

To cook the skewers, heat a barbecue grill plate or nonstick skillet over medium-high heat. Drizzle with a little extra oil. Cook the skewers for 2 to 3 minutes per side, or until cooked through. Serve warm with the warm satay sauce and sprinkled with diced red onion, cucumber and cilantro.

VIETNAMESE STEAMED PORK BUNS

Also known as *bánh bao*, this is a street food favorite in Vietnam. These fluffy white buns (*bao*) have a savory filling usually made of ground pork, onions and mushrooms, often seasoned with soy sauce and spices. They're steamed until soft and are perfect for a quick snack or light meal. With rich, complex flavor packed inside, each bite is a delightful experience. My recipe includes a hard-boiled quail egg and a slice of Chinese sausage as an extra treat. Whether you're familiar with these buns or looking to try something new, these buns offer a mouthful of flavors and textures that are sure to delight.

MAKES 12 BUNS

- -

Bao Bun Dough

3.5 oz (100 g) milk, at room temperature

3.5 oz (100 g) water, at room temperature

2 tbsp (26 g) sugar

1 tbsp (7 g) active dry yeast

10.5 oz (300 g) bun flour, plus more for dusting

Pinch of salt

Pork Mixture

7 oz (200 g) ground pork

0.75 oz (20 g) wood ear mushrooms, rehydrated in water, then chopped finely

4 water chestnuts, chopped finely

2 red shallots, chopped finely

2 spring onions, chopped finely

2 tbsp (20 g) fried shallots

1 tsp ground white pepper

½ tsp salt

1 tsp sugar

1 tsp oyster sauce

1 tsp Asian fish sauce

Filling

12 quail eggs (from a can)

1 Chinese sausage, sliced into 12 pieces

Make the bao bun dough: In a pitcher, combine the milk, water, sugar and yeast. Stir, then set aside for 5 minutes to activate the yeast. In the bowl of a stand mixer fitted with the dough hook, combine the bun flour and yeast mixture while mixing on low speed. Work up to medium speed and add the salt. Mix for 10 minutes, or until smooth. Cover the bowl with plastic wrap and set aside in a warm place to proof, approximately 30 minutes.

Make the pork mixture: In a medium-sized bowl, combine the pork, mushrooms, water chestnuts, red shallots, spring onions, fried shallots, white pepper, salt, sugar, oyster sauce and fish sauce, and mix well. Roll about ¼ cup (25 g) of the pork mixture into a ball, flatten it with the palm of your hand, then place a quail egg and a slice of Chinese sausage in the center. Wrap the mixture around to form a ball and set aside on a plate. Continue until all 12 pork balls are formed.

To finish shaping the buns, remove the dough from the bowl, reknead briefly and divide into 12 equal-sized portions. Roll out each portion into a circular wrapper 4 to 4¾ inches (10 to 12 cm) in diameter, using extra bun flour for dusting, if needed. Fill each wrapper with a pork mixture ball and pleat until your bun is sealed tight. Place each bun on a piece of parchment paper. Once all the buns are formed, cover with plastic wrap and let proof for 45 minutes. Line a bamboo steamer with parchment paper and place the steamer in a wok. Pour enough water into the wok for the water to reach 1 inch (2.5 cm) below the bottom of the steamer. Place the buns 1 inch (2.5 cm) apart in the steamer basket to allow them to expand. Steam over low heat for 10 to 12 minutes.

NOTE
- Bun flour can be found at your local Asian supermarket.

CHINESE PORK BURGER (ROU JIA MO)

Also known as the "Chinese hamburger," this is a beloved street food from China's Shaanxi province. Usually made with a flat, chewy bread known as *mo* that's generously filled with succulent, slow-cooked meat, my variation uses fluffy bao dough instead, which is lighter to eat but also helps hold in all those tasty juices. You can use any meat here, but my go-to is pork, as it remains tender and flavorful thanks to a mixture of spices like star anise as well as soy sauce. The next time you're entertaining, give this a crack instead of your classic pulled slider!

SERVES 10

- -

Buns
1 batch Bao Bun Dough (page 42)

Vegetable oil

Filling
1¾ lb (800 g) pork belly

5 slices fresh ginger

4 spring onions, cut into 1½" (4-cm) pieces

3 star anise

1 bay leaf

1 cinnamon stick

½ tsp fennel seeds

1 tsp Sichuan peppercorns

4 dried chile peppers

2 tbsp (30 ml) light soy sauce

1 tbsp (15 ml) dark soy sauce

1 tbsp (15 ml) Shaoxing rice wine

1 tbsp (13 g) sugar

1 tsp salt

For Serving
Handful of fresh cilantro, chopped

4 to 6 red chile peppers, chopped

Make the buns: Roll out the dough into a 1¼-inch (3-cm)-thick log and cut it into 10 equal-sized pieces. Roll each piece into a ball, using the palms of your hands. With a rolling pin, roll out each ball into a disk ⅛ inch (3 mm) thick or a little thicker, with a 4-inch (10-cm) diameter. Lightly brush the surface of the rolled-out dough with oil and gently fold in half. Transfer to a tray lined with parchment paper and cover with a clean, damp tea towel. Let the dough rise at room temperature, or until doubled in size. Line a bamboo steamer with parchment paper and place in a wok. Pour enough water into the wok for the water to reach 1 inch (2.5 cm) below the bottom of the steamer. Place the buns 1 inch (2.5 cm) apart in the steamer basket to allow them to expand. Steam over low heat for 8 to 10 minutes. This is optional, but once they're steamed, you can panfry your buns on both sides in a little oil to get a crisp golden exterior.

Cook the filling: Bring a medium- to large-sized pot of water to a boil. Add the pork belly and cook for 2 minutes before draining. Drain the pot and place the pork belly back in the pot along with the ginger, spring onions, star anise pods, bay leaf, cinnamon stick, fennel seeds, Sichuan peppercorns, chiles, light and dark soy sauces, wine, sugar and salt. Add just enough water to cover the pork belly completely. Bring to a boil, then lower the heat to low and simmer for 60 to 75 minutes, or until the meat becomes tender.

Remove from the heat and let cool to room temperature. Transfer the pork belly to a bowl and shred, using two forks. You may add a little bit of the cooking liquid back into this if you'd like it to be extra juicy. Toss with the cilantro and chiles, then portion into your bao buns.

SPICED CHICKEN MURTABAK

Murtabak is a culinary gem that beautifully captures the essence of street food. Originating from the Arabian Peninsula but wholeheartedly adopted and adapted by Southeast Asia, this savory pastry can be found on street corners in such countries as Malaysia, Singapore and Indonesia, each with their own unique spin on the classic. Imagine a thin, crispy dough pocket enveloping a tantalizing filling of ground chicken seasoned with a harmonious blend of spices, onions and eggs. The beauty of murtabak lies not just in its flavors but also in its versatility—and this is where my hack comes into play: Instead of making pastry from scratch, I've found using spring roll wrappers to be just as effective, making this dish an easy one to make in no time!

MAKES 4

- -

3 tbsp (45 ml) vegetable oil, divided

1 yellow onion, chopped finely

3 cloves garlic, chopped finely

1 tbsp (5 g) finely grated fresh ginger

1 tbsp (6 g) curry powder

1 tsp cumin seeds

10.5 oz (300 g) ground chicken

⅔ cup plus 1½ tsp (167 ml) water

Salt

2 large eggs

Handful of fresh cilantro, chopped finely

8 (8" [20-cm]) spring roll wrappers

1 large egg, beaten lightly, for brushing

Lime wedges, for serving

Sliced red onion, for serving

Make the chicken filling: In a medium-sized skillet, heat 1 tablespoon (15 ml) of the oil over high heat. Add the brown onion. Lower the heat to medium-low and cook, stirring often, for 5 minutes, or until the onion is soft. Add the garlic and ginger, and cook, stirring, for 1 minute, or until aromatic. Add the curry powder and cumin seeds, and stir to coat. Increase the heat to high. Add the ground chicken and cook, stirring, until browned. Add the water. Lower the heat to low and simmer for 20 minutes, or until the water has evaporated. Season with salt. Transfer to a bowl and set aside to cool. When cooled, stir in the eggs and cilantro.

To form, working with two sheets of pastry at a time, spoon ¼ cup (100 g) of the filling on one half, leaving a ⅜-inch (1-cm) bare margin all around. Brush the edge with the beaten egg, then fold over to seal. Repeat with the remaining pastry, filling and beaten egg.

Cook the murtabaks: In a large nonstick skillet, heat the remaining 2 tablespoons (30 ml) of oil over medium-high heat. Working in batches, carefully add the murtabaks and cook, turning often, for 5 minutes, or until crisp and golden. Drain on a paper towel. Allow to cool slightly before cutting into pieces. Serve with lime wedges and fresh red onion slices.

SPICY THAI BEEF BASIL (PAD GRA POW)

There is nothing more fitting in a book about street food than this iconic dish that captures the soul of Thai street food culture, perfectly balancing spicy, savory and a touch of sweet in every bite. Imagine walking through a bustling Thai market, where the aroma of sizzling meats and spices fills the air—that's the experience this dish brings to your table. In less than 30 minutes, you'll transform such simple ingredients as ground beef, Thai basil, garlic and chile peppers into a mouthwatering masterpiece. Serve it over steaming jasmine rice, and you've got a meal that's as comforting as it is exciting.

SERVES 2 OR 3

- -

2 tbsp (30 ml) vegetable oil

3 Thai bird chiles, or 2 long red chiles

3 shallots, sliced thinly

5 cloves garlic, chopped finely

17.5 oz (500 g) ground beef

1 tbsp (13 g) sugar

2 tbsp (30 ml) light soy sauce

1½ tbsp (23 ml) Asian fish sauce

⅓ cup + ½ tsp (83 ml) chicken stock

1 bunch Thai basil leaves

In a large skillet or wok over high heat, heat the oil. Once hot, add the chiles, shallots and garlic, and cook for 1 to 2 minutes, or until fragrant. Add the ground beef and stir, cooking until browned and making sure to break it up into smaller bits, about 5 minutes. Add the sugar, light soy sauce and fish sauce, and cook for an additional minute. Add the chicken stock to deglaze the pan, then stir in the Thai basil until wilted.

XINJIANG CUMIN LAMB STIR-FRY

This is a popular dish inspired by the flavors of Xinjiang, a region in northwest China known for its diverse culinary influences. The dish is a vibrant blend of bold flavors and textures, featuring lamb that's been marinated in a mix of aromatic spices, mostly cumin, adding an earthy, smoky aroma. The meat is then quickly stir-fried along with garlic, chiles and onion to create a smoky, spicy and incredibly flavorful dish. Serve this with steamed rice or noodles to balance the strong flavors!

SERVES 2 OR 3

Lamb

17.5 oz (500 g) leg of lamb, cut into 1" (2.5-cm) cubes

1 tbsp (15 ml) light soy sauce

1 tbsp (15 ml) Shaoxing rice wine

½ tsp salt

Rounded ¼ cup (35 g) cornstarch

Spice Mixture

2 tbsp (14 g) ground cumin

2 tsp (3 g) red pepper flakes

½ tsp sugar

¼ tsp ground Sichuan pepper

Stir-Fry

2 to 4 tbsp (30 to 60 ml) vegetable oil, divided

½ cup + 2 tsp (39 g) dried red chile peppers

1 tsp minced fresh ginger

4 to 5 cloves garlic, sliced

1 small onion, sliced

1 bunch cilantro, chopped

Toasted white sesame seeds, for garnish

Marinate the lamb: In a bowl, combine the lamb, soy sauce, wine and salt, and toss until well coated. Cover and refrigerate to marinate for 30 minutes or overnight. Once marinated, remove from the fridge and mix in the cornstarch until well coated.

Make the spice mixture: In a small bowl, combine the cumin, red pepper flakes, sugar and Sichuan pepper, then set aside.

To cook, in a large skillet or wok, heat 2 to 3 tablespoons (30 to 45 ml) of oil over medium-high heat. Add the lamb pieces, spreading them out, and cook until golden, about 1 minute. Flip and cook the other side for another minute. Transfer the lamb to a plate and add another tablespoon (15 ml) of oil to the pan. Add the dried chiles, ginger and garlic, and stir-fry until fragrant, about 1 minute. Add the onion and stir-fry for an additional minute. Add the lamb back to the pan and sprinkle with the spice mixture. Toss until well combined and adjust the seasoning to taste. To finish, toss with the chopped cilantro and transfer to your serving dish. Garnish with sesame seeds.

SPICY MAURITIAN CHICKEN CURRY

This heartwarming dish is special to me. It reminds me of my childhood, and when I cook it, I like to do it just how Grandmère does, with a whole chicken. What sets this dish apart is its unique combination of spices—including fenugreek, cumin and cinnamon—complemented by the sweetness of onions and the tang of tomatoes. It's a dish that you'll find at both family gatherings and local eateries across Mauritius, each version carrying the signature touch of the cook who made it. Whether you serve it with fragrant rice, roti or even a side of pickled vegetables, this curry is more than just a meal. It's a celebration of Mauritian culture and tradition.

SERVES 4 TO 6

----

3 tbsp (45 ml) vegetable oil

1 onion, chopped

1 tbsp (10 g) minced garlic

1½ tsp (3 g) minced fresh ginger

1 sprig thyme

10 to 12 curry leaves

5 green cardamom pods

5 cloves

2 cinnamon sticks

2 dried red chile peppers

1 tbsp (6 g) cumin seeds

1 tbsp (6 g) fenugreek seeds

7 oz (200 g) tomatoes, chopped

4¼ cups (1 L) plus 2 tbsp (30 ml) water, divided

5 tbsp (30 g) garam masala

1 (4½-lb [2-kg]) chicken, cut into pieces

4 medium-sized potatoes, peeled and quartered

Salt

Fresh cilantro, for garnish

In a large saucepan, heat the oil over medium heat. Add the onion and cook until softened, 3 to 5 minutes. Add the garlic, ginger, thyme, curry leaves, cardamom, cloves, cinnamon, dried chiles and the cumin and fenugreek seeds. Lower the heat to low and cook, stirring, for 10 minutes.

Add the tomatoes, 2 tablespoons (30 ml) of water and the garam masala. Simmer and cook, stirring, until a paste is formed. Add the chicken pieces, potatoes and the remaining 4¼ cups (1 L) of water. Increase the heat to medium-high and bring to a boil, then lower the heat to medium-low and simmer for 30 to 40 minutes, or until the chicken is cooked and tender. Season with salt to taste, then remove from the heat and serve garnished with fresh cilantro.

GRILLED LEMONGRASS PORK CHOP

This isn't your run-of-the-mill pork chop dish; it's a celebration of Vietnamese flavors. Think: juicy pork chops infused with a delicious marinade consisting of lemongrass, garlic and other seasonings. When these chops hit the grill, the direct heat helps caramelize the marinade, turning it into crispy, charred perfection. When that citrusy lemongrass aroma fills the air, you just know you're in for something special! You can slice and serve this pork chop wrapped in lettuce leaves, but I like to eat it with steamed rice, a *nuoc cham* dipping sauce and fresh herbs.

SERVES 4

- -

Grilled Pork Chop

2 lemongrass stalks, white part only, sliced

3 cloves garlic, minced

Juice of 2 limes

¼ cup (60 ml) Asian fish sauce

2 tbsp (30 ml) light soy sauce

¼ cup (60 g) dark brown sugar

2 tbsp (30 ml) grapeseed oil

26.5 oz (750 g) thinly cut pork chops, preferably blade end, with plenty of fat and marbling

Nuoc Cham

3 cloves garlic, minced

Juice of 1 lime

2 tbsp (30 ml) distilled white vinegar

¼ cup (60 ml) Asian fish sauce

3 tbsp (39 g) granulated sugar

1 red chile pepper

½ cup + 1 tsp (125 ml) water

For Serving

Steamed rice

2 cucumbers, sliced into rounds

Butter lettuce leaves

Fresh cilantro leaves

Marinate the pork: In a medium-sized bowl, combine the lemongrass, garlic, lime juice, fish sauce, light soy sauce, brown sugar and grapeseed oil, and stir well. Place the pork chops in a large bowl and pour the marinade over them. Use your hands to rub the marinade evenly over the pork chops. Cover and refrigerate for 1 hour or overnight.

Make the nuoc cham: In a small bowl, combine the garlic, lime juice, vinegar, fish sauce, granulated sugar, chile and water, and stir until the sugar has completely dissolved into the sauce. Taste and adjust any of the ingredients, if desired.

Heat a barbecue grill to high and, discarding the marinade, cook the marinated pork chops for 4 to 6 minutes on each side, or until golden brown. Remove and serve with the nuoc cham for dipping, rice, cucumbers, butter lettuce leaves and cilantro.

THREE

SEAFOOD

Hey, sea-foodies, welcome to the chapter that's all about embracing the ocean's bounty—Asian street food style! If you love the sweet, briny flavors of seafood, this chapter's going to reel you in—hook, line and sinker. I'm diving deep into the culinary seas to bring you some serious flavor waves, with mouthwatering recipes. Now, where do I start . . .

Picture yourself wandering along a seaside market in Asia, where the catch of the day turns into culinary masterpieces right before your eyes. You might want to start your journey with Cantonese Salt and Pepper Squid (page 60)—a dish so crispy and flavorful, it's like a beach party in your mouth. It's simple, but boy, does it pack a punch with my addition of such aromatics as garlic, spring onion and chile.

Then, hop over to Korea for some Crispy Korean Seafood Pancake (page 68). Imagine a medley of seafood nestled in a savory, crispy pancake creating a harmony of delicious textures. Trust me, it's a dish that screams comfort and will make you feel like you're at a bustling Korean market.

And then there's the showstopper: Singapore Chile Crab (page 76). Rich, spicy and loaded with succulent crabmeat, this dish is a culinary icon for a reason. You might think it's complicated, but I've got some kitchen hacks that'll make cooking this luxe dish a breeze.

The best part? With my help and a few handy tricks up your sleeve, these seafood delights (and many more) are totally doable at home. No need for fancy gadgets or inaccessible ingredients; we're all about making it easy-peasy while keeping flavors on point. So ready your skillets—we're about to turn your kitchen into the ultimate Asian seafood shack!

FRIED OYSTER OMELET

Taiwanese oyster omelet is a beloved street food classic that has locals and tourists lining up at night markets across the island. Now, it might not sound like a worthy match, but I assure you this combination of ocean-fresh oysters and a slightly gooey, eggy batter is quite delicious. The point of difference here is that when sweet potato starch is mixed in with the batter, it all comes together in a hot wok, crisping up into a golden, half-crispy, half-gooey masterpiece. But what really elevates it is the sauce—a sweet and sour concoction including soy and ketchup. Drizzled on top, it transforms the omelet into a saucy, savory delicacy that's irresistibly moreish.

SERVES 2

Oyster Omelet

4 large eggs

¼ tsp salt

¼ tsp ground white pepper

2 tbsp (30 ml) vegetable oil

6 to 8 small oysters, shucked

Sweet potato starch slurry (⅓ cup [80 ml] water mixed with 1 tbsp [10 g] sweet potato starch)

⅓ cup (5 g) celery leaves or fresh cilantro leaves

1 spring onion, sliced, for garnish

Sweet and Sour Sauce

¼ cup (60 ml) ketchup

¼ cup (60 ml) rice vinegar

1 tbsp (13 g) sugar

1 tsp light soy sauce

Cornstarch slurry (½ cup [120 ml] water mixed with 1½ tsp [4 g] cornstarch)

Salt

Make the oyster omelet: In a medium-sized bowl, combine the eggs, salt and white pepper. Whisk well and set aside. Place a large nonstick skillet over high heat and add the vegetable oil. When the oil is hot, add the oysters and cook until they firm up, about 1 minute. Pour in the egg mixture and let cook until the bottom has just set, about 30 seconds. Pour the sweet potato starch slurry over the egg mixture and, using a spatula, gently pull the egg mixture toward the center from the edges to mix the two batters slightly, then spread out to form a circular omelet 4 to 4¾ inches (10 to 12 cm) in diameter. Cook until golden brown on the bottom for 2 to 3 minutes, top with celery leaves, then carefully flip, cooking for an additional 2 to 3 minutes on the other side. Transfer to a serving dish.

Make the sweet and sour sauce: In a small saucepan, combine the ketchup, rice vinegar, sugar and light soy sauce. Place over medium-high heat, stir and bring to a simmer until the sugar dissolves, about 2 minutes. While stirring, pour in the cornstarch slurry and continue to cook until thickened, about 2 minutes. Season with salt as desired and remove from the heat.

Drizzle the omelet with the sweet and sour sauce, and garnish with spring onion.

CANTONESE SALT AND PEPPER SQUID

This dish embodies the sublime simplicity of Asian street food while also transcending cultural boundaries to be a global favorite. Found in menus all around the world, this culinary delight is a perfect blend of two basic seasonings: salt, which is a cornerstone in cuisines around the world, and pepper, the fiery counterpart that adds a kick to the palate. But don't be fooled by the simplicity of its name; when these humble ingredients meet high-quality, tender squid, culinary magic happens. Once the squid is fried, I like to stir-fry it with such aromatics as garlic, chile and spring onion, for extra flavor.

SERVES 4

- -

Squid

24.7 oz (700 g) squid tentacles and hoods, cleaned

1 tbsp (15 ml) Shaoxing rice wine

½ tsp sesame oil

1 tbsp (15 ml) vegetable oil, plus more for frying

5 cloves garlic, sliced

2 long red chiles, sliced

2 spring onions, sliced

½ tsp salt

½ tsp sugar

¼ tsp ground white pepper

¼ tsp ground Sichuan pepper

Flour Mixture

½ cup (60 g) all-purpose flour

½ cup (38 g) semolina

⅓ cup (58 g) uncooked polenta

1 tsp salt, plus more to taste

½ tsp ground white pepper, plus more to taste

To prepare the squid, cut the tentacles into bite-sized pieces. Cut the squid hood in half lengthwise, then score a crisscross pattern on the inside, using a sharp knife. Cut into 1¼-inch (3-cm) squares. Pat dry with a paper towel, then combine in a bowl with the wine and sesame oil. Cover with plastic wrap and place in the fridge to marinate for at least 20 minutes.

Meanwhile, make your flour mixture: In a large bowl, stir together the flour, semolina, polenta, salt and white pepper.

Fill a wok with vegetable oil about two-thirds of the way up. Heat over high heat to 350°F (180°C) and test by dipping a wooden chopstick into the oil; the chopstick will sizzle when the oil is ready. Remove the squid from the fridge, dredge in the flour mixture, then deep-fry until golden brown, 2 to 3 minutes. Transfer to a baking sheet lined with paper towels, to drain.

Place another wok over medium-high heat and add the 1 tablespoon (15 ml) of vegetable oil. Add the garlic, chiles and spring onions, and stir-fry for 30 seconds, or until aromatic. Add the squid along with the salt, sugar, white pepper and Sichuan pepper. Toss gently to combine and infuse all the flavors. Serve immediately.

JAPANESE CRAB CROQUETTES (KOROKKE)

Imagine diving into a crispy, golden-brown morsel and discovering an indulgent filling of pure, succulent crabmeat, beautifully seasoned and expertly cooked. This is Japanese crab *korokke*, a luxurious take on the traditional Japanese croquette. While most korokke recipes feature a potato or meat base, this crab-centric version skips the spuds to let the sweet and briny flavors of the crab truly shine with corn kernels and an indulgent béchamel sauce to tie it all together. Perfect as an appetizer, this croquette brings the irresistible allure of Japanese street food straight to your kitchen!

MAKES 8

Croquettes

2 tbsp + ½ tsp (30 g) unsalted butter

½ onion, chopped finely

⅓ cup (75 g) canned corn, drained

5.5 oz (150 g) crabmeat (canned)

¼ cup (31 g) all-purpose flour

Scant ⅞ cup (200 ml) whole milk

¼ tsp salt

¼ tsp freshly ground black pepper

2 tbsp (15 g) grated Cheddar cheese

Batter

3 tbsp + 1 tsp (50 ml) cold water

1 large egg

½ cup + 2 tbsp (75 g) all-purpose flour, divided

1⅔ cups (100 g) panko bread crumbs

Vegetable oil

Korokke Sauce

2 tbsp (30 ml) ketchup

1 tbsp (15 ml) Worcestershire sauce

Make the croquettes: In a medium-sized saucepan, melt the butter over medium-low heat. Add the onion and cook until soft and translucent, 2 to 3 minutes. Add the corn and crabmeat, and cook, stirring, for 1 minute. Add the flour and stir until well incorporated. Slowly pour in the milk while whisking until smooth, 2 to 3 minutes. Add the salt, pepper and cheese. Cook, stirring until thick and creamy, 4 to 5 minutes. Pour the mixture into a deep baking pan, cover with plastic wrap and freeze for 30 minutes, or until firm.

Make the batter: In a small bowl, whisk together the cold water, egg and half of the flour until smooth. Place the remaining flour in a shallow bowl and the panko in another. Remove the crab filling from the freezer and cut into eight equal-sized portions. Using your hands, roll each portion into a barrel shape. Coat the crab barrels with flour, followed by the batter and then a generous amount of panko. Use your hands to press the crumbs onto each croquette.

Fry the croquettes: Fill a wok with vegetable oil about two-thirds of the way up. Heat to 350°F (180°C) over high heat and test by dipping a wooden chopstick into the oil; the chopstick will sizzle when the oil is ready. Working in batches, gently lower the croquettes into the oil and fry until crispy and golden brown, 3 to 5 minutes. Transfer to a plate lined with paper towels, to drain.

Meanwhile, make the korokke sauce: In a small bowl, stir together the ketchup and Worcestershire.

Serve the croquettes with the korokke sauce.

TAIWANESE PARTY PRAWNS

This dish captures the essence of Taiwanese street food culture—bold flavors, simple ingredients and a fun, social eating experience—they're the life of the party! Picture this: succulent prawns, lightly battered then deep fried until crisp and golden, sitting on a bed of pineapple slices and topped with sweet mayonnaise and a shower of colorful sprinkles. You might think sprinkles are just for desserts, but this creation proves that they can bring unexpected joy to savory dishes, too. It takes your typical seafood appetizer to a whole new level of fun while also being delicious!

SERVES 2 OR 3

Sweet Mayo

Rounded ⅓ cup (78 g) mayonnaise

1½ tbsp (23 ml) fresh lemon juice

1 tbsp (13 g) sugar

1 tbsp (15 ml) heavy cream

Crispy Prawns

17.5 oz (500 g) raw prawn tails, shelled, deveined

½ tsp salt

¼ tsp ground white pepper

2 large egg whites, beaten lightly

1 rounded cup (166 g) potato starch

Vegetable oil

For Serving

1 rounded cup (78 g) shredded lettuce leaves

4 slices canned pineapple, drained, cut into chunks

Hundreds and thousands sprinkles, to garnish

Make the sweet mayo: In a small bowl, stir together the mayonnaise, lemon juice, sugar and cream, then refrigerate until ready to serve.

Make the crispy prawns: Butterfly each prawn by scoring along the back where the vein is, using a sharp knife. Place in a bowl and season with the salt and white pepper. Toss well, then stir in the beaten egg whites. Place the potato starch in a separate shallow bowl.

Fill a wok with vegetable oil about two-thirds of the way up. Heat to 350°F (180°C) over high heat and test by dipping a wooden chopstick into the oil; the chopstick will sizzle when the oil is ready. Working in batches, carefully dredge the prawns in the potato starch before lowering them into the hot oil. Deep-fry for 1½ minutes before transferring to a plate lined with paper towels, to drain. Once all the prawns are fried, fry a second time for another 1½ minutes, or until crisp and golden brown. Drain again on paper towels.

To serve, scatter the shredded lettuce on your serving dish, followed by the pineapple chunks and crispy prawns. Drizzle with a generous amount of sweet mayo and top with the hundreds and thousands sprinkles. Serve immediately.

CREAMY TUNA EGG SANDWICH

When you think of Asian street food, sandwiches might not be the first thing that comes to mind. But hold on to your culinary hat, because sandwiches have taken the streets of countries like China and Japan by storm, offering a fascinating blend of Eastern and Western flavors. This particular sandwich has been a simple comfort food classic for me while traveling. Imagine biting into soft, pillowy bread and immediately being met with a rich, creamy tuna filling balanced out with fresh, crunchy lettuce. Perfect for picnics, for lunch boxes or even as a no-fuss dinner, this sandwich is as versatile as it is delicious. Feel free to change it up by adding different spices and fresh herbs.

SERVES 4

Eggs

2 tbsp (30 ml) vegetable oil

4 large eggs

Salt and freshly ground black pepper

4 lettuce leaves

Tuna Mayo Mixture

½ medium-sized onion, chopped finely

10.5 oz (300 g) canned tuna in brine, drained

6 tbsp (84 g) Japanese mayonnaise, such as Kewpie® brand

¼ tsp freshly ground black pepper

½ tsp salt

8 slices thickly sliced white sandwich bread

Cook the eggs: In a large nonstick skillet, heat the oil in the pan over medium-low heat. Carefully crack the eggs into the pan and let cook slowly until the egg whites are just set, about 3 minutes. Season with a pinch each of salt and pepper, and remove from the heat. Set aside.

Make the tuna mayo mixture: In a medium-sized bowl, stir together the onion, tuna, mayonnaise, pepper and salt, then set aside.

Assemble your sandwiches: For each sandwich, place a lettuce leaf on one slice of bread. Top with one fried egg and one-quarter of the tuna mayo mixture. Top with another slice of bread, then slice in half.

CRISPY KOREAN SEAFOOD PANCAKE

Otherwise known as *pajeon*, this is a comfort food of Korean street markets. A crispy, savory pancake studded with a medley of seafood and spring onions is not your average pancake; it's a flavor-packed dish that promises an explosion of flavors—and the unique tang of the dipping sauce takes it to the next level. Whether you're enjoying it as a hearty snack or as an appetizer before a Korean BBQ feast, it's a versatile treat that everyone can get behind. I like to place it at the center of the table and let everyone tear pieces off with their chopsticks, embodying the communal spirit of Korean dining.

SERVES 4

- -

Seafood Pancake

1 scant cup (120 g) all-purpose flour

2 tbsp (16 g) cornstarch

1 cup + 2 tsp (250 ml) soda water, chilled

1 tsp Asian fish sauce

1 bunch spring onions, cut into 1½" (4-cm) lengths

2 tbsp (30 ml) vegetable oil

13 oz (375 g) mixed raw seafood (squid, prawns and mussels)

2 large eggs, lightly beaten

Dipping Sauce

2 tbsp (30 ml) light soy sauce

1 tbsp (15 ml) rice vinegar

1 tbsp (15 ml) water

2 tbsp (20 g) finely chopped onion

1 tsp minced garlic

1 tsp gochugaru (Korean chili flakes)

Make the pancake: In a medium-sized bowl, stir together the flour and cornstarch, then whisk in the soda water and fish sauce until well combined. Add the spring onions and mix well.

In a large skillet, heat the oil over medium heat. Spoon in half of the pancake batter and spread until thin. Let cook for 1 to 2 minutes, or until the edges are just set, then sprinkle with half of the seafood mixture. Drizzle over half of the beaten egg and, using a spatula, spread the beaten egg evenly across the pancake. Continue to cook for an additional 1 to 2 minutes, or until the bottom is crisp and golden brown, then carefully flip the pancake with your spatula and cook for an additional 1 to 2 minutes, or until the other side is golden brown. Transfer to a chopping board and repeat with the remaining pancake batter. Cut into 1¼- to 1½-inch (3- to 4-cm)-wide pieces and serve with the following dipping sauce.

Make the dipping sauce: In a small bowl, stir together the light soy sauce, rice vinegar, water, onion, garlic and gochugaru until well combined.

HONG KONG CURRY FISH BALLS

Fish balls are a popular food item in various Asian cuisines, often featured as street food but also served in casual and fine dining settings. These tasty spheres are typically made from fish that has been finely ground or minced, then mixed with such ingredients as starch, salt and other seasonings. Curry fish balls, a skewered version found piping hot and soaked in a rich, aromatic curry sauce, are the epitome of Hong Kong street food culture. They're more than just a quick bite; they're a hug for your palate. So grab a skewer (or two) and let's bring the spirit of Hong Kong's vibrant streets right into your kitchen!

SERVES 4

2 tbsp (30 ml) vegetable oil

3.5 oz (100 g) finely chopped red onion

2 cloves garlic, minced finely

1 tsp minced fresh ginger

Fresh curry leaves from 8 sprigs

1 tbsp (6 g) curry powder

½ tsp ground turmeric

2 cups + 2 tbsp (500 ml) chicken stock

1 tbsp (15 ml) light soy sauce

1 tbsp (15 ml) Asian fish sauce

1 tbsp (13 g) sugar

Salt, to taste

1 lb (450 g) daikon, cut into 1¼" (3-cm) chunks

21 oz (600 g) fried fish balls

Cornstarch slurry (2 tbsp [16 g] cornstarch mixed with 3 tbsp [45 ml] water)

Make the curry sauce: In a large saucepan, heat the oil over medium heat. When hot, add the onion and cook until softened and translucent, 2 to 3 minutes. Add the garlic, ginger and curry leaves, and cook for an additional 2 minutes, or until fragrant. Add the curry powder and turmeric, and cook, stirring, for another minute. Mix in the chicken stock and bring to a boil. Lower the heat to low and simmer for 15 minutes. Add the light soy sauce, fish sauce, sugar and salt to taste. Add the daikon, mix well and cook until soft, about 5 minutes. Finally, add the fish balls and let them cook and soak up the sauce, about 2 minutes.

While simmering, thicken the sauce by whisking in the cornstarch slurry. Continue to cook and stir for an additional 2 to 3 minutes. Serve immediately.

NOTE

- Fried fish balls are available at most Asian specialty grocery stores.

GRILLED SAMBAL RED SNAPPER

Spice lovers, rejoice! *Sambal* fish is here to awaken your senses and bring the heat straight to your dining table—or should I say, re-create that magical experience you'd get from a bustling hawker stall in Southeast Asia. Imagine a perfectly cooked fish, its flaky texture complementing the robust, spicy sambal sauce that clings to every bite. Now, I know this recipe mentions red snapper, which I am lucky enough to have access to in Western Australia, but any sweet and flaky fish will do. I've also enjoyed this dish with stingray in Singapore, so if you can use that, even better! Have fun, give this a go and I assure you, the savory, spicy, sweet flavors will be sure to tantalize your taste buds.

SERVES 2

Sambal Paste

4 red chile peppers, sliced in half and seeded

2 shallots, peeled and halved

4 tsp (20 g) toasted shrimp paste

1 lemongrass stalk, white part only, sliced thinly

¼ tsp salt

2 tsp (10 ml) Asian fish sauce

2½ tsp (10 g) sugar

Juice of 1 lime

8 tbsp (120 ml) vegetable oil, divided

Fish Parcel

2 (7-oz [200-g]) red snapper filets

Ground turmeric, for dusting

4 banana leaves (about 9¾" x 9¾" [25 x 25 cm])

Lime wedges, for serving

Soy Vinegar Dipping Sauce

1 shallot, sliced finely

3 Thai bird's eye chiles, sliced

2 tbsp (30 ml) light soy sauce

1 tbsp (15 ml) distilled white vinegar

Make the sambal paste: In a blender, combine the chile peppers, shallots, shrimp paste, lemongrass, salt, fish sauce, sugar, lime juice and 1 tablespoon (15 ml) of oil and blend on high speed until a paste is formed. In a saucepan, heat about ⅓ cup plus 4 teaspoons (100 ml) of vegetable oil over medium heat. Add the sambal paste and cook, stirring, for about 10 minutes, or until fragrant.

Cook the fish: Pat a filet dry and dust with turmeric on both sides. Spread the cooked sambal paste evenly over both sides and place on a banana leaf. Cover with the second banana leaf and use two bamboo skewers to hold the leaves together by piercing and weaving at two ends. Repeat this step for the second filet, using two additional skewers.

Heat a griddle pan or barbecue grill over high heat. Once hot, place the parcels on the griddle or grill and cook for 10 minutes. Serve with lime wedges and the following dipping sauce.

Make the dipping sauce: In a small bowl, stir together the shallot, chiles, light soy sauce and vinegar.

NOTE

- If you can't source snapper, then sea bass, halibut and perch are all great substitutes.

STEAMED FISH WITH SPRING ONION AND GINGER

Get ready to be transported to a place of culinary bliss with one of my favorite comfort foods: steamed flaky whole fish adorned with aromatic spring onion and ginger and drizzled with a touch of light soy sauce. Whether you're at a family gathering or delighting in the authenticity of a hawker stall, this dish is a universal crowd-pleaser. Now, I know this dish often graces tables during Lunar New Year, but don't wait for a special occasion; the beauty of it all lies in its simplicity, making it perfect for any day you'd like to turn into an occasion. So, gather around, breathe in its delicious aroma and savor this timeless classic that pays homage to the fine art of Asian cooking.

SERVES 2

---

3 tbsp (45 ml) light soy sauce

½ tsp sugar

1 tbsp (15 ml) water

1 whole fish, cleaned and scaled (about 17.5 oz [500 g])

5 to 7 spring onions, white part only, 4 to 6 cut into 4" (10-cm) lengths, for steaming fish, 2 sliced into thin matchsticks

Generous 1 oz (30 g) fresh ginger, sliced into thin matchsticks

3 tbsp (45 ml) vegetable oil

Fresh cilantro leaves, for serving

Make the sauce for the fish: In a small saucepan over medium heat, combine the light soy sauce, sugar and water. Cook, stirring, until the sugar has dissolved, about 1 minute. Remove from the heat and set aside.

Pat the fish dry and make two or three slits about 1 inch (2.5 cm) deep on both sides where the flesh is the thickest. On a heatproof platter that fits onto a wok, place the white part of the spring onions across the platter, followed by the fish on top. The spring onion will stop the fish skin from sticking to the platter as it steams.

Pour enough water in a wok for the water to reach 2 inches (5 cm) deep. Add a rack that fits above the water, and once the water is boiling, add the platter with its fish. Steam for 12 to 14 minutes, or until the fish is just cooked through. Remove the platter from the wok and carefully pour off any liquid. Drizzle with the sauce and scatter the thinly sliced spring onion and ginger on top.

In a small saucepan, heat the vegetable oil in a small pan until hot and starting to smoke, then carefully pour over the spring onion and ginger to sizzle. Garnish with fresh cilantro leaves and serve immediately.

NOTE

- Sea bass, sea bream, snapper and barramundi are all great fish to use. This recipe can also be made with filets instead of whole fish. Best served with freshly steamed jasmine rice.

SINGAPORE CHILE CRAB

Roll up your sleeves and get ready for a finger-licking extravaganza. This is an iconic dish that captures the essence of Singaporean cuisine. Now, if you haven't tried it, imagine tender crabmeat coated in a vibrant sweet, spicy and umami sauce thanks to the magical mix of tomato, chiles and soy. Whether you find yourself savoring it at a local hawker stall or re-creating the magic in your own kitchen, the experience is quintessentially Singaporean. Yes, that's right—making this dish at home is not only doable but equally rewarding. It's messy, it's communal and it's utterly delicious. So, grab a group of friends and dig into a culinary adventure that'll leave your taste buds tingling and your heart yearning for more!

SERVES 4

2 whole fresh mud crabs (about 17.5 oz [500 g] each)

⅓ cup + 4 tsp (100 ml) vegetable oil

3 shallots, chopped finely

2 tbsp (20 g) minced garlic

2 tbsp (10 g) minced fresh ginger

4 Thai bird's eye chiles, chopped finely

2 cups + 2 tbsp (500 ml) chicken stock

Rounded ¼ cup (68 g) tomato paste

½ cup + 1 tsp (146 g) sweet chili sauce

Salt, to taste

Sugar, to taste

Cornstarch slurry (1 tbsp [8 g] cornstarch mixed with 2 tbsp [30 ml] water)

1 large egg, beaten

3 spring onions, sliced

Fresh cilantro leaves, for garnish

Prepare the mud crabs: Remove the flap at the back to pull off the hard shell. Next, lay the crab upside down on your chopping board and use a cleaver to cut it in half along the midline. Carefully remove the gut and gills with your fingers and rinse. Try to keep any crab mustard from this part. Portion the crab by dividing the rest of the body into three or four pieces, using the cleaver. Carefully crack the hard claws and legs with a rolling pin. This will help them absorb the sauce and make them easier to eat later on.

Cook the sauce: In a large lidded wok, heat the oil over medium-high heat. When hot, add the shallots, garlic, ginger and chiles, and cook uncovered, stirring, until fragrant, about 2 minutes. Add the crab pieces and crab mustard along with the chicken stock and increase the heat to bring to a boil. Cover loosely with the lid and let cook until the crab is just cooked through, about 5 minutes. Remove the lid and stir in the tomato paste and sweet chile sauce. Season with salt and balance out with sugar, to taste. Stir in the cornstarch slurry and cook to thicken until a gravylike consistency is reached. Stir in the beaten egg until just cooked, and add the spring onions. Transfer to a serving plate and garnish with fresh cilantro leaves.

FOUR

VEGETARIAN

Welcome to the world of vegetarian street food! If you think veggies are just sides, then brace yourself—this chapter's about to change the game. I'm shining the spotlight on some kick-butt meat-free dishes that don't play second fiddle to anyone. I'm talking about such dishes as Panfried Turnip Cake (*Lo Bak Go*) (page 81), Sichuan-Style Veggie Wontons (page 86), Spiced Potato Fritter Buns (*Vada Pav*) (page 94) and many more! Let me give you a little taster . . . .

The turnip cake isn't your grandma's vegetable cake; this is a savory, umami-packed delight often found in dim sum joints but also on the bustling streets of cities like Hong Kong and Taipei. With crispy edges and a soft, chewy center, it's a dish that can convert even the staunchest veggie skeptics. I can't tell you how many times I've ordered this along the side of the road for a quick and tasty breakfast!

In this chapter, I also venture to the spicy and aromatic world of Sichuan cooking with my veggie wontons. Imagine a bundle of joy filled with vegetables and seasonings, swimming in a spicy, garlicky sauce. It's a taste explosion that'll have your taste buds doing a happy dance, changing the way you look at wontons and dumplings!

And I can't forget to make a pit stop to the streets of Mumbai for some potato fritter buns. Think of them as India's answer to the burger but with spiced potato. It's street food royalty, and it's about to become your new obsession, just as it became mine after a trip to India in 2023.

Now for the great news: With my step-by-step guidance and kitchen hacks, these recipes are a cinch to make at home. I promise you don't need to be a five-star chef to pull off these dishes—just have a love of good food and a willingness to try something new. Have some fun and cook these for your friends and fam, proving that vegetarian dishes can be the star of any culinary show!

PANFRIED TURNIP CAKE (LO BAK GO)

Step aside, potato gratin; turnip cake (also known as radish cake) is here to steal the spotlight! This Cantonese delicacy is a perfect blend of the humble and the sublime. Crafted from grated Chinese turnip (*lo bok*) or daikon as well as rice flour and a medley of umami-rich ingredients like shiitake mushrooms, each bite is a burst of flavors and textures. You'll often find this panfried wonder gracing the tables of dim sum parlors, but did you know it's also a beloved item in Taiwanese street food and breakfast spots? Crispy on the outside and tender on the inside, it transcends cultural and culinary boundaries. And guess what? It's easier to make at home than you might think. A few simple steps and you're on your way to enjoying this classic dish right from the comfort of your own kitchen!

SERVES 4

4 tbsp (30 ml) vegetable oil, divided, plus more for loaf pan

2 cloves garlic, finely chopped

1 shallot, chopped finely

6 dried shiitake mushrooms, rehydrated and chopped

4 spring onions, chopped

2 lb (900 g) Chinese radish or daikon, peeled and grated

1½ tsp (9 g) salt

1 tsp ground white pepper

1 tsp sesame oil

2 tbsp (30 ml) vegetarian oyster sauce

1½ tsp (9 g) mushroom or vegetable bouillon powder

Rice flour batter (8 oz [225 g] rice flour mixed with 1½ cups + 1 tbsp [370 ml] water)

Sriracha or chili sauce, for serving

Make the turnip cake: In a wok, heat 2 tablespoons (30 ml) of the vegetable oil over medium heat. Add the garlic and shallot, and stir-fry for 2 minutes, or until fragrant. Add the shiitake mushrooms and spring onions, and stir-fry for an additional 2 to 3 minutes. Add the grated radish, stir and cover. Cook for 10 minutes, or until the turnip has softened and liquid is being released. There will be enough liquid for the turnip to start boiling. Stir in the salt, white pepper, sesame oil, vegetarian oyster sauce and mushroom bouillon. Slowly add the rice flour batter while stirring, and cook for about 2 minutes, or until thickened and pastelike in consistency.

Pour the batter into a well-oiled 9 x 5–inch (23 x 12.5–cm) loaf pan and steam over medium-high heat for about 45 minutes. Remove from the steamer once cooked and let set for about 30 minutes. Once cool, cut into 1-inch (2.5-cm) cubes.

In a large nonstick skillet, heat the remaining 2 tablespoons (30 ml) of vegetable oil over medium heat. Cook the cubes until golden and crisp on two sides, 6 to 8 minutes. Serve with Sriracha.

FRIED OYSTER MUSHROOMS

Prepare to be swept off your feet by the crunchy, umami-packed taste of fried oyster mushrooms! This recipe turns the humble mushroom into an addictive crispy snack that'll have you reaching for more. Coated in a light batter and kissed by hot oil until golden brown, these mushrooms are the epitome of simple ingredients transformed into something so wonderfully tasty. Perfect as an appetizer, a side or even the star of your meal, this dish is as versatile as it is delicious. And if you've ever wandered through hawker stalls or a street food market, you'll know this fried delight is a shared love across various culinary landscapes. Now, why should you make this at home? Because it's incredibly easy to prepare and offers a restaurant-quality experience right at your own dining table.

SERVES 2

Mushrooms

10.5 oz (300 g) oyster mushrooms

6 tbsp (72 g) potato starch

½ tsp salt

½ tsp Chinese five-spice powder

Vegetable oil

Salt and ground white pepper

Spicy Mayo

1 cup + 2 tsp (234 g) Japanese mayonnaise, such as Kewpie brand

3 tbsp (45 ml) Sriracha

For Serving

Fresh cilantro leaves

Carefully tear the oyster mushrooms apart into smaller pieces, using your hands. Place in a medium-sized bowl along with the potato starch, salt and five-spice powder. Toss until well combined and evenly coated.

Fill a wok with vegetable oil about two-thirds of the way up. Heat to 350°F (180°C) over high heat and test by dipping a wooden chopstick into the oil; the chopstick will sizzle when the oil is ready. Working in batches, carefully fry the coated mushrooms until crisp and golden brown, 4 to 5 minutes. Transfer to a baking sheet lined with paper towels, to drain. Sprinkle it with extra salt and white pepper, to your liking.

Make the spicy mayo: In a small bowl, stir together the mayonnaise and Sriracha in a small bowl until well combined.

Serve the mushrooms with the spicy mayo and cilantro leaves.

GRILLED VEGETABLE SKEWERS

Who says you need meat to enjoy the smoky, umami-rich pleasures of yakitori? By substituting traditional chicken or pork with an array of flavorful vegetables, including eggplant, mushrooms and shishito peppers, this dish is a celebration of clean eating without sacrificing taste. Picture vegetable skewers coated in a mouthwatering *tare* sauce and grilled to perfection. Whether you're a vegetarian, a flexitarian or just looking for a healthier twist on a favorite, this dish is for you. Making yakitori at home is a fun and rewarding experience, perfect for impressing guests or even treating yourself. So, grab some skewers, fire up that grill and let's turn your kitchen into a plant-based *izakaya* (Japanese tapas bar)!

SERVES 4

Tare Sauce
½ cup (120 ml) light soy sauce
½ cup (120 ml) mirin
¼ cup (60 ml) sake
2 tbsp (26 g) sugar
3 spring onions, white part only
1 clove garlic
1 slice fresh ginger

Vegetables
1 Japanese eggplant
1 zucchini
8 shiitake mushrooms
24 shishito peppers
24 cherry tomatoes
8 asparagus stalks

Soak 36 bamboo skewers in water for 30 minutes.

Make the tare sauce: In a small saucepan over medium heat, combine the soy sauce, mirin, sake, sugar, spring onion white parts, garlic and ginger. When the mixture comes to a boil, lower the heat to low and simmer, stirring, until thickened and glossy, 15 to 20 minutes. Discard the spring onion, garlic and ginger from the sauce and remove the sauce from the heat.

Cut all the vegetables into bite-sized pieces that can be threaded onto your skewers. Thread four to six vegetable pieces on each skewer, alternating the vegetables for a colorful presentation.

To cook, place the vegetable skewers on a hot grill and let cook, flipping occasionally, until lightly charred, 5 to 6 minutes. Brush generously with the tare sauce on all sides and continue to grill for an additional 2 to 3 minutes, or until caramelized.

SICHUAN-STYLE VEGGIE WONTONS

Dumpling lovers, meet your new best friend! These silky pockets of flavor offer a roller coaster ride for your taste buds, combining the earthy richness of mushrooms with the electrifying kick of spicy Sichuan sauce. You might discover them at a bustling market or a tucked-away Sichuan eatery. You can easily replicate this culinary gem right at home with a handful of ingredients and fresh store-bought wonton wrappers; it's ideal for anyone looking to up their cooking game and explore the wonders of Sichuan cuisine.

MAKES 30 TO 35 WONTONS

Wontons

2 tbsp (30 ml) vegetable oil

2 cups (250 g) shredded carrot

2 cups (185 g) shredded cabbage

7 oz (200 g) shiitake mushrooms, chopped finely

4 spring onions, chopped

1 tbsp (10 g) minced garlic

2 tsp (4 g) minced fresh ginger

2 tbsp (30 ml) light soy sauce

2 tbsp (30 ml) vegetarian oyster sauce

1 tsp sesame oil

1 tsp ground white pepper

30 to 35 wonton wrappers

Spicy Sichuan Dressing

1 tbsp (15 ml) light soy sauce

2 tbsp (30 ml) Chinese black vinegar

2 tbsp (30 ml) chili oil

1½ tsp (6 g) sugar

½ clove garlic, grated finely

1 tbsp (3 g) chopped spring onion

1 tbsp (1 g) chopped fresh cilantro

1 tsp toasted white sesame seeds

For Serving

Fresh cilantro leaves

Spring onion, sliced

Make the wonton filling: In a wok, heat the oil over medium heat. Add the carrot, cabbage and mushrooms, and stir-fry for 6 to 8 minutes, or until the vegetables have softened and all the liquid has cooked out. Stir in the spring onions, garlic, ginger, light soy sauce, vegetarian oyster sauce, sesame oil and white pepper. Cook for an additional 2 to 3 minutes. Transfer to a bowl, taste and adjust the seasoning as desired. Let cool completely before using.

Assemble the wontons: Place a teaspoon of filling in the center of one wrapper. Brush half of the edges of the square with water. Fold the wet edges over (in half lengthwise) to create a rectangular shape that encloses the filling. Brush one of the corners with water and fold it over to overlap with the other corner. Press to seal. Repeat, using the remaining wrappers and filling. Set aside, covered with a clean, damp tea towel.

Make the spicy Sichuan dressing: In a small bowl, stir together the light soy sauce, black vinegar, chili oil, sugar, garlic, spring onion, cilantro and sesame seeds until the sugar has dissolved.

Cook the wontons in a pot of boiling water until cooked through, 3 to 4 minutes. Using a slotted spoon, remove from the water and divide among serving bowls. Serve immediately with a generous amount of the dressing and garnish with cilantro leaves and sliced spring onion.

BRAISED FIVE-SPICE TOFU (LU WEI)

Lu wei is a comforting dish that harmonizes layers of flavor into a single mouthwatering experience. Whether you've encountered it in a bustling Taiwanese night market or in a traditional Chinese eatery, the memory lingers. This tofu delicacy marries the warmth of such spices as star anise and cinnamon with the hearty richness of soy sauce. Slow cooked to perfection, the tofu, shiitake and radish soak up these complex flavors like a sponge, delivering a satisfying bite every time. The best part: It's surprisingly easy to make at home, perfect for weeknights and special occasions alike. Re-create the magic in your own kitchen, and you'll realize that this is more than a dish—it invites you to slow down and savor each bite.

SERVES 2 TO 3

1 tbsp (15 ml) vegetable oil

3 slices fresh ginger

1 cinnamon stick

3 star anise pods

3 bay leaves

½ tsp fennel seeds

1 tsp Chinese five-spice powder

1 tsp ground white pepper

½ tsp freshly ground black pepper

2 tbsp (30 ml) light soy sauce

1 tbsp (15 ml) dark soy sauce

1 tbsp (13 g) sugar

8½ cups (2 L) water

6 shiitake mushrooms

7 oz (200 g) daikon, cubed

7 oz (200 g) firm tofu, cubed

7 oz (200 g) fried tofu, cubed

Salt, to taste

½ tsp sesame oil

In a large saucepan, heat the oil over medium heat. Add the ginger, cinnamon stick, star anise pods, bay leaves and fennel seeds, and sauté until fragrant, 1 to 2 minutes. Add the five-spice powder, white and black pepper, light soy sauce, dark soy sauce, sugar and water. Stir until well combined. Bring to a boil, then add the shiitake mushrooms, daikon, firm tofu and fried tofu, and let simmer for 30 minutes. Season to taste with salt and the sesame oil.

SWEET AND SPICY CAULIFLOWER (GOBI MANCHURIAN)

This ultimate fusion dish unites the best of Indian and Chinese flavors. Imagine crispy fried cauliflower florets drenched in a spicy, tangy sauce made with a medley of soy sauce, garlic and chile—each bite is a burst of contrasting textures and bold tastes. It's as perfect for a festive gathering as for a cozy dinner. The cherry on top? This addictive Indo-Chinese marvel is a breeze to whip up at home.

SERVES 2 TO 3

- -

Cauliflower

Florets from 1 cauliflower head

¾ cup (90 g) all-purpose flour

¼ cup (33 g) cornstarch

½ tsp chili powder

½ tsp ground ginger

½ tsp ground garlic

¼ tsp salt

½ cup + 1 tsp (125 ml) water

Vegetable oil

Manchurian Sauce

2 tbsp (30 ml) vegetable oil

2 cloves garlic, chopped finely

1 (1" [2.5-cm]) piece fresh ginger, chopped finely

2 green chile peppers, cut in half

¼ onion, chopped finely

¼ cup (14 g) chopped spring onion

2 tbsp (30 ml) ketchup

1 tsp Sriracha

1 tbsp (15 ml) distilled white vinegar

1 tbsp (15 ml) light soy sauce

½ cup + 1 tsp (125 ml) water

¼ tsp freshly ground black pepper

¼ tsp salt

Cornstarch slurry (1 tsp cornstarch mixed with 1 tbsp [15 ml] water)

Sliced spring onion, for garnish

Blanch the cauliflower: Bring a large pot of well-salted water to a boil over high heat and cook the cauliflower florets for 1 to 2 minutes—it should still be crunchy. Drain and run under cold water to stop the cooking. Drain well and set aside.

Make the cauliflower batter: In a medium-sized bowl, stir together the flour, cornstarch, chili powder, ginger, garlic and salt, then add the water and stir again until well combined. Toss in the blanched cauliflower and stir to coat.

Fill a wok with vegetable oil about two-thirds of the way up. Heat to 350°F (180°C) over high heat and test by dipping a wooden chopstick into the oil; the chopstick will sizzle when the oil is ready. Working in batches, gently lower the coated cauliflower into the oil and cook until crispy and golden brown, 2 to 3 minutes. Transfer to a plate lined with paper towels, to drain.

Make the Manchurian sauce: In a large skillet or wok, heat the oil over medium-high heat. Add the garlic, ginger and green chile, and stir-fry until fragrant, about 1 minute. Add the onion and spring onion, and stir-fry for about 2 minutes. Stir in the ketchup, Sriracha, vinegar, light soy sauce, water, black pepper and salt, and cook, stirring, for 1 minute. While stirring, pour in the cornstarch slurry and cook until the sauce thickens and turns translucent. Stir in the fried cauliflower to coat with the sauce, then transfer to your serving dish. Garnish with spring onion.

PANFRIED CABBAGE AND GLASS NOODLE BUNS

Welcome to the world of panfried buns—a twist on the traditional panfried dumpling—that's bigger and just as delectable as it is versatile. Imagine pillowy steamed buns filled with an aromatic mixture of cabbage and glass noodles, their underside seared to crispy perfection. It's the kind of dish that feels like a warm hug from your favorite auntie at a bustling street stall in Asia. And, trust me: Making these at home is not just rewarding but also a whole lot of fun—perfect for a cooking date or a family kitchen adventure. So, grab your chopsticks and prepare to indulge in the comforting goodness of Panfried Cabbage and Glass Noodle Buns!

MAKES 12 BUNS

3.5 oz (100 g) uncooked mung bean vermicelli (a.k.a. glass noodles)

3 tbsp (45 ml) vegetable oil, divided, plus more as needed

½ large head cabbage, shredded

4 spring onions, chopped

1 tbsp (15 ml) light soy sauce

Salt

1 tbsp (8 g) toasted white sesame seeds

2 tbsp (30 ml) toasted sesame oil

1 batch Bao Bun Dough (page 42)

Make the filling: Prepare the vermicelli according to the instructions on the package. Once cooked, drain, then roughly chop into ⅜-inch (1-cm)-long pieces. In a large skillet or wok, heat 2 tablespoons (30 ml) of vegetable oil over medium to medium-high heat. When hot, add the cabbage and spring onions. Stir-fry until tender, 8 to 10 minutes, then add the vermicelli and toss to coat. Season with the light soy sauce and salt to taste, then stir in the toasted white sesame seeds and sesame oil. Remove from the heat and let cool.

Shape the buns: Divide the dough into 12 equal-sized portions. Roll out each portion into a circular wrapper 4 to 4¾ inches (10 to 12 cm) in diameter, using extra bun flour for dusting if needed. Fill with the cabbage filling and pleat until your bun is sealed tight. Place on a tray lined with parchment paper. Repeat until all the buns are formed.

Cook the buns: In a large nonstick skillet with a lid, heat 1 tablespoon (15 ml) of vegetable oil over medium-high heat. Add the buns, seam side down. Cook, uncovered, until the underside of the buns is golden brown, then add a scant ½ cup (120 ml) of water and cover with lid. Cook for 8 to 10 minutes, or until risen and cooked through. Remove the lid and continue to cook until the pan is dry and the underside of the buns are crisp again. If needed, add additional oil to help crisp them up. Serve immediately.

NOTE
- You may flip the buns and panfry them on the other side, for extra crispiness.

SPICED POTATO FRITTER BUNS (VADA PAV)

This iconic Mumbai sandwich is comfort food at its finest—a spicy potato fritter enveloped in a soft bun, slathered with an array of chutneys and spices. When you bite into the fluffy bun and hit the crispy vada, your taste buds dance to the tune of garlic, tamarind and cilantro. Assemble it at home with friends or family and you've got yourself a meal that's as enjoyable to prepare as it is to eat!

MAKES 8 BUNS

- -

Cilantro Chutney

1 rounded cup (17 g) chopped cilantro leaves

2 cloves garlic, chopped

1 tbsp (15 ml) fresh lemon juice

1½ tsp (8 ml) tamarind concentrate

2 green chile peppers, chopped

Salt, to taste

Potato Filling

12.5 oz (350 g) russet potatoes, peeled

2 tbsp (30 ml) vegetable oil

½ tsp mustard seeds

10 curry leaves

6 garlic cloves, minced

2 green chile peppers, minced

Pinch of ground turmeric

1 tbsp (1 g) chopped cilantro leaves

Salt, to taste

Batter

1 cup + 1 tsp (125 g) besan flour (a.k.a. garbanzo flour)

⅛ tsp ground turmeric

½ tsp baking soda

½ tsp salt

½ cup + 1 tsp (125 ml) water

For Serving

8 round dinner rolls

Sambal oelek (found at most Asian grocers)

Make the cilantro chutney: In a food processor, combine the cilantro, garlic, lemon juice, tamarind concentrate, green chiles and salt to taste with a little water, and process until smooth. Set aside.

Make the potato filling: Boil the potatoes until soft, then mash in a heatproof bowl. In a large skillet, heat the oil over medium heat, then add the mustard seeds. Let crackle before adding the curry leaves and doing the same. Add the garlic, green chiles and turmeric, then stir and cook for an additional 30 seconds, or until fragrant. Pour this mixture into the mashed potato and stir, adding the chopped cilantro and salt to taste. Form eight equal-sized balls with your hands, cover and set aside.

Make the batter: In a small bowl, combine the besan flour, turmeric, baking soda, salt and water, and stir until smooth.

Fill a wok with vegetable oil about two-thirds of the way up. Heat to 350°F (180°C) over high heat and test by dipping a wooden chopstick into the oil; the chopstick will sizzle when the oil is ready. Working in batches, dip the potato balls in the batter to coat, then fry until crisp and golden brown on all sides, 2 to 3 minutes. Transfer to a plate lined with paper towels, to drain.

To assemble, slice a bread roll in half, then spread on the cilantro chutney and sambal oelek to taste. Add a potato fritter and serve immediately.

MAURITIAN SPLIT PEA FLATBREAD (DHAL PURI)

Get ready to be transported straight to the vibrant streets of Mauritius with *dhal puri*! This iconic Mauritian flatbread holds a special place in my heart; it's a dish that echoes the warmth and tradition of my family. While I was growing up, its scent filling the air meant comfort, love and a hearty meal to look forward to. At its core, this is a soft, thin wrap filled with ground yellow split peas, but what makes it truly unforgettable is its versatility. Enjoyed with hot sauce, a dollop of Cilantro Chutney (page 94) or some Butter Bean Curry (page 115), each bite is a new adventure. Grab your rolling pin and get ready to discover the soul of Mauritian cuisine, one dhal puri at a time!

MAKES APPROX. 20

---

1 cup (225 g) uncooked yellow split peas

½ tsp cumin seeds

4 cups (507 g) all-purpose flour, plus more for dusting

½ tsp ground turmeric

1 tsp salt

1½ to 2 cups (355 to 480 ml) water

Vegetable oil

Cilantro Chutney (page 94), for serving

Chili sauce or Sriracha, for serving

Make the dhal puri: Soak the yellow split peas in water overnight, then drain and rinse. In a small skillet, toast the cumin seeds over medium heat for about 2 minutes, then crush with a mortar and pestle or spice grinder. Boil the drained yellow split peas in salted water until just cooked through and tender, 15 to 20 minutes. Drain and transfer to a food processor along with the toasted cumin. Blend and set aside until required.

Make the dough: In a large bowl, stir together the flour, turmeric and salt. Slowly pour in the water while stirring, until a rough dough is formed. Transfer to a flour-dusted work surface and knead until smooth, about 5 minutes. Cover with a clean, damp tea towel and let rest for 30 minutes.

To form the wraps, divide the dough into portions the size of a golf ball and use your thumb to make an indentation in the center of each ball. Stuff with 1 tablespoon (15 to 20 g) of the yellow split pea mixture and seal by pressing and pinching the dough around the filling. Using extra flour to dust, roll out each wrap to about ⅛ inch (3 mm), or a little less, thick.

To cook, place a large skillet over medium heat and brush with the oil. Working one at a time, cook each dhal puri for about 2 minutes on each side, or until the pastry is cooked but not browned. Serve warm with cilantro chutney and chili sauce.

MALAYSIAN SPICY FRUIT SALAD (ROJAK)

Rojak is a quintessential Southeast Asian salad that dances on the fine lines between sweet, spicy and umami. This is a fruit salad, but not as most people know it. Forget the predictable combination of orange slices and grapes—rojak features a symphony of tropical fruits offset by crisp veggies and other surprise elements, such as crispy tofu, dressed with a tantalizing tamarind sauce. It's a dish that thrives on diversity, mirroring the melting pot of cultures in places like Singapore, Malaysia and Indonesia. Every time I eat this, it never fails to surprise and delight with every mouthful being so different. And don't be daunted—making it is forgiving and flexible. Grab a bowl, have some fun and let your taste buds wander!

SERVES 4

- -

Rojak Sauce

12 dried chile peppers

½ cup + 1 tsp (125 ml) water

1 cup + 2 tsp (250 ml) sweet soy sauce

1 cup + 2 tsp (250 ml) sweet chili sauce

½ cup + 1 tsp (125 g) ketchup

Rounded ¼ cup (62 g) dark brown sugar

2 tsp (12 g) salt

Salad

7 oz (200 g) turnip or radish

7 oz (200 g) cucumber

7 oz (200 g) pineapple

7 oz (200 g) bean sprouts, blanched

7 oz (200 g) guava or green apple

2 youtiao (Chinese donut sticks)

7 oz (200 g) fried tofu

10.5 oz (300 g) roasted peanuts, chopped

2 tbsp (16 g) toasted white sesame seeds

Make the rojak sauce: Wash the dried chiles, then soak in boiling water for 30 minutes. Drain and transfer to a food processor with the water. Blitz until smooth. Transfer to a large skillet over medium heat along with the sweet soy sauce, sweet chili sauce, ketchup, brown sugar and salt. Cook for 5 minutes, stirring, or until thick, then set aside to cool.

Make the salad: Peel and chop all the fruit and vegetables into 1- to 2-inch (2.5- to 5-cm) cubes and combine in a large bowl. Preheat the oven to 375°F (190°C). On a baking sheet lined with parchment paper, bake the Chinese donut sticks and fried tofu for 10 to 15 minutes, or until crispy. Chop into 1- to 2-inch (2.5- to 5-cm) pieces and add to the bowl of fruit. Add the rojak sauce and toss until all the ingredients are well coated, then transfer to a serving dish. Scatter roasted peanuts and toasted sesame seeds over the top.

FIVE

APPETIZERS & SNACKS

This chapter is for the snack enthusiasts out there—welcome to what might just be my favorite part of the book: street food appetizers and snacks! If you're anything like me, you love the idea of sampling a little bit of everything. Small bites, big flavor—that's what this chapter's all about. I'm diving into a smorgasbord of tasty treats that'll tickle your taste buds and make your next gathering a hit, with such dishes as Mauritian Chili Fritters (*Gateaux Piment*) (page 108), Japanese Egg Rice Ball (*Onigiri*) (page 112) and Black Pepper Beef Buns (*Hu Jiao Bing*) (page 120)!

Mauritian Chili Fritters is a nod to my roots. These spicy lentil fritters are tiny but mighty, loaded with flavors that'll transport you straight to the beaches of Mauritius. They're perfect as a snack or paired with some delicious hot sauces. I've enjoyed them time and time again with my family—and now you can, too!

I also want to make a special mention of my *onigiri*, a delightful Japanese rice ball with a hidden gem inside—a tasty, seasoned egg. It's portable, customizable and oh so delicious. It might sound simple, but trust me, you'll wanna make a batch every week!

Last but definitely not least, meet the star of Taiwanese bakeries and street food stalls: *hu jiao bing*. These buns pack a peppery beef filling encased in crispy, moreish dough. They're perfect for pleasing a crowd or just satisfying your own snack cravings.

And, don't worry, I've got your back. With my kitchen hacks and easy-to-follow instructions, you'll be serving up these appetizing wonders like a seasoned street food vendor. These recipes are fantastic for entertaining; they're conversation starters, tummy fillers and mood lifters all in one. So, grab your shopping list and fire up your kitchen, because you're about to snack your way through Asia without leaving home.

POTATO AND BEEF SAMOSA

This samosa recipe brings together the earthy richness of beef and the comforting goodness of spiced potatoes, all encased in a crispy, golden triangular shell. Similar to empanadas or turnovers, yet distinctly Indian in flavor with such aromatic spices as coriander and cumin, these samosas serve as a bridge between cultures and culinary traditions. And here's my special tip, borrowed from my Grandmère: To make life a bit easier without compromising on flavor, use spring roll pastry instead of making the dough from scratch. It's also worth making a large batch and freezing them, because once you've tried this delicious parcel, you'll want to be going back for more!

MAKES APPROX. 24 SAMOSAS

- -

2 russet potatoes, peeled

17.5 oz (500 g) ground beef

1 large red onion, chopped finely

2 tsp (6 g) minced garlic

2 tsp (4 g) minced fresh ginger

1 tsp freshly ground black pepper

1 tomato, chopped

2 tsp (4 g) ground coriander

2 tsp (4 g) mild curry powder

1 tsp garam masala

1 tsp ground turmeric

1 tsp salt

2 tbsp (30 ml) vegetable oil, plus more for frying

1 medium-sized onion, chopped finely

2 green chile peppers, chopped finely

1 bunch fresh cilantro, chopped finely

3 spring onions, chopped finely

10 to 12 curry leaves, chopped finely

1 (18-oz [500-g]) package spring roll pastry, thawed

Flour glue (2 tbsp [15 g] all-purpose flour mixed with 2 tbsp [30 ml] water)

Make the filling: Boil the potatoes until tender, then mash and set aside. In a pressure cooker, combine the beef with the red onion, garlic, ginger, black pepper, tomato, ground coriander, curry powder, garam masala, turmeric and salt. Place on high pressure for 10 minutes, then remove the lid and continue to cook until there is no more liquid. In a medium-sized skillet, heat 2 tablespoons (30 ml) of oil over medium-high heat and sauté the onion and green chiles, about 2 minutes. Add the cooked beef mixture and continue to cook for 2 minutes. Taste and season as desired, then remove from the heat and mix with the mashed potato, fresh cilantro, spring onions and curry leaves.

Form the samosas: Slice the spring roll pastry into thirds to make long rectangular sheets. Keep them covered with a clean, lightly damp tea towel to stop them from drying out. Working with one sheet at a time, fold the end in to form a triangular shape. Brush a little flour glue onto the excess pastry and tuck underneath to stick, forming a triangular pouch. Fill with 1 heaping tablespoon (20 to 25 g) of filling and continue to fold the long end over. Brush some more flour glue to seal your samosa.

To cook, fill a wok with vegetable oil about two-thirds of the way up. Heat to 350°F (180°C) over high heat and test by dipping a wooden chopstick into the oil; the chopstick will sizzle when the oil is ready. Working in batches, carefully fry the samosas until crisp and golden brown, 2 to 3 minutes. Transfer to a baking sheet lined with paper towels, to drain. Serve immediately.

VIETNAMESE CRISPY PORK BÁNH MI

Bánh mi is a Vietnamese sandwich that packs a punch in every bite. My version includes golden slices of pork mingling with a medley of crunchy pickles, fresh veggies and herbs, zesty hoisin, a rich mayo and—most important—pâté. Making this at home is easier than you think with my air-fryer pork belly hack; and trust me, one bite will transport you straight to the bustling streets of Saigon.

SERVES 6

- -

Crispy Air-Fryer Pork Belly

1 (scant 3½-lb [1.5-kg]) piece pork belly, skin on

1 tbsp (18 g) salt, plus more for sprinkling

5 star anise pods

5 cloves

3 bay leaves

1 tsp Chinese five-spice powder (optional)

Pickle Mix

1 carrot, peeled and grated with a julienne peeler

½ daikon, peeled and cut into ⅜" (1-cm)-square batons as long as your rolls

2 tbsp (36 g) salt

½ cup + 1 tsp (125 ml) water

½ cup + 1 tsp (125 ml) distilled white vinegar

Rounded ¼ cup (52 g) sugar

For Serving

6 crusty bread rolls

6 tbsp Vietnamese pâté

½ cup + 2 tsp (117 g) Japanese mayonnaise, such as Kewpie brand

Hoisin sauce

2 cucumbers, sliced

Red chile peppers, sliced

Fresh cilantro

Make the crispy pork belly: Make slits on the meat side of the pork belly, about 1 inch (2.5 cm) apart. In a medium-sized pot, combine 13 cups (3 L) of water and the salt, star anise pods, cloves, bay leaves and if using, five-spice powder, and place over high heat. Bring to a boil, add the pork belly, lower the heat slightly and let cook for 35 minutes. Once cooked, remove the pork belly, pat dry and pierce the skin all over with a fork. Season the pork belly with salt, then place, skin side up, in an air fryer and air fry at 400°F (200°C) for 25 to 30 minutes, or until the skin is crackling. Remove and let cool slightly before slicing (you can use the slits underneath to help slice).

Make the pickle mix: In a bowl, toss the carrot and daikon with the salt, and let sit for 30 minutes. Rinse, drain, then combine in a medium-sized bowl with the fresh water, vinegar and sugar. Cover and refrigerate.

Assemble the bánh mi: Spread the rolls with 1 tablespoon pâté each, Japanese mayonnaise and a little hoisin sauce. Fill with slices of pork belly, pickle mixture (drained), cucumber, red chile slices and cilantro.

PORK BELLY STEAMED BUN (GUA BAO)

Where do I even start? Picture this: melt-in-your-mouth, juicy slices of pork belly enveloped in a fluffy, steamed bun. Now, add some pickled mustard greens, fresh cilantro and roasted peanuts, and you've got yourself a pocket of pure heaven. These Taiwanese street food favorites, often called "Taiwanese hamburgers," are the epitome of comfort food. Now, if you don't have time to make the bao buns from scratch, you can easily source these at an Asian grocer—cutting down the cooking time by more than half. It's a dish that not only wows your taste buds but also paints a vivid picture of Taiwan's bustling night markets, all from the comfort of your own home, so make sure to give it a go for yourself!

MAKES 10 TO 12 BAO BUNS

----

1 tbsp (15 ml) vegetable oil, plus extra for brushing

17.5 oz (500 g) pork belly, sliced into ⅝" (1.5-cm)-thick slabs

3 to 4 cloves garlic, chopped

2 to 3 slices fresh ginger

2 spring onions, cut into 2" (5-cm) pieces

1 star anise pods

1 cinnamon stick

3 tbsp (45 ml) Shaoxing rice wine

2 tbsp (30 ml) light soy sauce

1 tbsp (15 ml) dark soy sauce

1 tbsp (15 g) dark brown sugar

3 cups + 2 tbsp (740 ml) water

For Serving

1 batch Bao Bun Dough (page 42)

Chopped pickled mustard greens

Fresh cilantro

Chopped roasted peanuts

Make the pork belly: In a large skillet, heat the oil over medium-high heat. Once hot, brown the pork belly slabs on both sides for about 2 minutes, then remove from the heat and set aside. Keeping the same pan on the heat, add the garlic, ginger and spring onions, cooking until fragrant, about 2 minutes. Add the star anise pods, cinnamon, wine, light soy sauce, dark soy sauce, brown sugar and water. Stir until well combined. Add the pork and bring to a boil, then lower the heat to a simmer for about 60 minutes, or until the pork is tender but still holding its shape. Strain the cooking liquid and place it back in its pan over the heat, cooking until it has thickened, about 15 minutes. Slice the pork belly into 2-inch (5-cm) pieces and add it to the reduced sauce, tossing until well coated. Set aside.

Form the bao buns: Shape the dough into a ⅛-inch (3-mm)-thick log and cut into 10 to 12 equal-sized pieces. Roll each piece into a ball and allow to rest for 3 minutes. Roll out each ball until ⅛ inch (3 mm) thick or slightly thicker, and use a 4-inch (10-cm) round cookie cutter to trim each into a circle. Lightly brush the surface of the rolled-out dough with oil and gently fold in half. Transfer to a tray lined with parchment paper and cover with a clean, damp tea towel. Let the dough rise at room temperature until doubled in size, 30 to 60 minutes.

Steam the bao buns: Line a bamboo steamer with parchment paper and place the steamer in a wok. Pour enough water into the wok to reach 1 inch (2.5 cm) below the bottom of the steamer. Place the buns 1 inch (2.5 cm) apart in the steamer basket to allow them to expand. Steam over medium heat for 8 to 10 minutes.

Once the buns are steamed, open them up gently and fill them with pickled mustard greens and braised pork belly, then top with fresh cilantro and roasted peanuts. Serve immediately.

MAURITIAN CHILI FRITTERS (GATEAUX PIMENT)

Gateaux piment, which translates to "chili cake," is Mauritius's answer to falafel. Made from a hearty blend of split peas, fresh chile peppers and aromatic spices, these little fried wonders are anything but ordinary. They're crunchy on the outside and delectably tender on the inside, leaving you reaching for more. Perfect as a grab-and-go snack from a street vendor or as an appetizer to kick off a festive meal, this is easy to make at home. So, why not add a touch of island magic to your kitchen with this crispy morsel? One bite and you'll see why this snack has captured hearts far beyond the shores of Mauritius.

MAKES ABOUT 20 FRITTERS

Scant 9 oz (250 g) dried yellow split peas

½ onion, chopped finely

2 spring onions, chopped

Handful of fresh cilantro, chopped

6 curry leaves, chopped

4 red chile peppers, chopped finely

½ tsp cumin seeds

Salt, to taste

Vegetable oil

Chili sauce or Sriracha, for serving

Soak the yellow split peas in water overnight to soften. Drain and rinse under water. Drain again. Transfer the split peas to a food processor and process on low speed until a chopped, grainy texture is achieved. Transfer to a medium-sized bowl and add the onion, spring onions, cilantro, curry leaves, chiles and cumin seeds. Season with salt to taste and mix well. Using your hands, roll into small bite-sized balls and set aside on a tray.

Fill a wok with vegetable oil about two-thirds of the way up. Heat over high heat to 350°F (180°C) and test by dipping a wooden chopstick into the oil; the chopstick will sizzle when the oil is ready. Working in batches, carefully fry the split pea balls until crisp and golden brown, 4 to 5 minutes. Transfer to a baking sheet lined with paper towels, to drain. Sprinkle with extra salt and serve immediately with chili sauce on the side, for dipping.

FRESH PRAWN RICE PAPER ROLLS

These Vietnamese-inspired beauties are like little parcels of joy, packed with succulent prawns, crisp veggies and aromatic herbs. Wrapped in translucent rice paper, they're as pleasing to the eye as they are to the palate. Don't forget to dip them in my rich peanut sauce for an extra layer of deliciousness that elevates the whole experience. Now, I know everyone loves the classic crispy spring roll, but these rice rolls are a fresh alternative, perfect for a light lunch or dinner while offering a guilt-free indulgence that's big on flavor. What I love most is that they're a breeze to make and so much fun to assemble!

MAKES 12 ROLLS

- -

Rice Paper Rolls

18 cooked prawns, shelled and deveined

3 oz (85 g) thin rice vermicelli

12 edible rice paper sheets

Butter lettuce leaves

1 carrot, peeled and cut into thin matchsticks

1 Persian cucumber, cut into matchsticks

½ cup (20 g) fresh mint leaves

Peanut Sauce

½ cup + 1 tsp (133 g) peanut butter

½ cup + 1 tsp (125 ml) water

2 tbsp (30 ml) rice vinegar

2 tbsp (30 ml) light soy sauce

2 tbsp (30 ml) honey

1 tsp sesame oil

Make the spring rolls: Slice the prawns in half horizontally. Bring a pot of water to a boil over high heat, then add the vermicelli noodles and remove from the heat, leaving them in the water to soak and soften for about 5 minutes. Then, drain and run under cold water to stop the cooking.

Form the rice paper rolls: Fill a large shallow dish with lukewarm water. Lay a clean, damp tea towel over a chopping board. Briefly dip a sheet of rice paper in the water, ensuring the entire surface area is wet. Place a piece of butter lettuce close to the bottom of the rice paper sheet and add a pinch each of noodles, carrot, cucumber and mint. Top with three pieces of prawn and roll up the rice paper slightly to ensure the filling is covered and a log shape is being formed. Tuck in the edges and continue to roll until completely rolled into a log. Repeat the process until all the rolls are formed. Serve with the peanut sauce.

Make the peanut sauce: In a small bowl, stir together the peanut butter, water, rice vinegar, light soy sauce, honey and sesame oil until well combined.

JAPANESE EGG RICE BALL (ONIGIRI)

This is no ordinary *onigiri*! While traditional rice balls often feature such fillings as pickled plum or grilled salmon, my version takes a beloved breakfast staple—the soft-boiled egg— and tucks it into the heart of the rice, offering a delightful surprise with every bite. Onigiri is a versatile snack that you can find anywhere from street food stalls to convenience stores like 7-Eleven across Japan. Eating it takes me back to my childhood, when a simple bowl of egg and rice would often be my go-to dinner on nights when there was nothing else to eat. Perfect for snacking or as part of a bento box, this dish delivers a meal that's both nourishing and tasty.

MAKES 8 ONIGIRI

- -

Dashi

1 kombu sheet

1 oz (30 g) bonito flakes

Shoyu Tare

1 cup + 2 tsp (250 ml) soy sauce

2 tsp (10 ml) sake

2 tsp (10 ml) mirin

1 tsp sugar

1 tsp minced garlic

Scant 1½ tsp (3 g) minced fresh ginger

1 spring onion

1 small piece kombu

1 oz (30 g) bonito flakes

Eggs

4 large eggs, at room temperature

Rounded 1 cup (208 g) uncooked sushi rice

For Assembly

8 tsp (40 ml) Japanese mayonnaise, such as Kewpie brand, for serving

Furikake

Make the dashi: In a medium-sized saucepan, bring 4 cups (946 ml) of water to a boil over high heat. Add the kombu sheet, lower the heat to medium-low and simmer for 10 minutes. Remove the pot from the heat and add the bonito flakes. Cover and let sit for 10 minutes, strain, then keep the liquid.

Make the *shoyu* tare: In a small saucepan, combine the soy sauce, sake, mirin, sugar, garlic, ginger, spring onion, small piece of kombu and bonito, and bring to a boil over high heat. Lower the heat to low, simmer for 10 minutes, then strain and set aside to cool.

Soft-boil the eggs: Bring a small pot of water to a boil over high heat. Add the eggs (in their shell) and let boil for 5 minutes. Remove the eggs and drop into ice cold water to stop the cooking, then drain and peel. Place the peeled eggs in a container with 2 tablespoons (30 ml) of the shoyu tare and turn to allow the marinade to coat the eggs. Cover and refrigerate to marinate overnight, then remove from the marinade and slice in half.

Cook the rice: In a medium-sized saucepan with a lid, combine the sushi rice, 1½ cups + 1 tablespoon (370 ml) of the dashi stock and 1 tablespoon (15 ml) of the shoyu tare over high heat. Bring to a boil, lower the heat to a simmer and cover with the lid. Cook for 15 minutes, or until the rice is cooked through and tender. Remove from the heat, remove the lid and fluff the rice with a fork. Let cool slightly before forming the onigiri.

Form the onigiri: Fill a 2⅜- to 2¾-inch (6- to 7-cm)-diameter round cookie cutter with rice. Scoop out enough from the center to fit one egg half in the rice. Squeeze in 1 teaspoon of mayo and carefully add the other egg half, cut side up. Remove the cookie cutter and roll the bottom part of the onigiri in *furikake*. Repeat to form the remaining onigiri.

ROTI CANAI WITH BUTTER BEAN CURRY

Welcome to the wonderful world of roti canai, Malaysia's beloved flatbread that's taken the global food scene by storm! Crispy on the outside and soft and fluffy on the inside, this grilled bread is a masterpiece of textures and flavors. Although it's delicious enough to be enjoyed on its own, it's also the ideal item for soaking up sauces such as a simple butter bean curry that I personally adore. While it's a staple in Malaysian *mamak* stalls, the beauty of roti canai is that it can be replicated at home with a bit of practice and flair. So, roll up your sleeves and get ready to be transported to the streets of Kuala Lumpur with every bite!

MAKES 10 FLATBREADS

Roti Dough

18 oz + 2 tsp (520 g) bread flour

1 tsp salt

Scant 3 tbsp (40 g) unsalted butter, melted

1 large egg, at room temperature

1 tbsp (15 ml) sweetened condensed milk

1¼ cups + 2 tsp (310 ml) water

Vegetable oil

Butter Bean Curry

2 tbsp (30 ml) vegetable oil

1 onion, chopped finely

2 tsp (6 g) minced garlic

1 tsp minced fresh ginger

1 tsp mild curry powder

½ tsp ground cumin

½ tsp ground turmeric

½ tsp ground coriander

7 oz (200 g) canned tomatoes, crushed

14 oz (400 g) canned butter beans, drained and rinsed

1 cup + 2 tsp (250 ml) vegetable stock

¾ cup + 1½ tsp (182 ml) coconut milk

Salt, to taste

Make the roti dough: In the bowl of a stand mixer fitted with the dough hook, combine the bread flour, salt, melted butter, egg, sweetened condensed milk and water. Mix at medium speed until a dough is formed, about 10 minutes. Let rest for 5 minutes, then knead again for an additional 5 minutes. Divide the dough into 10 equal-sized portions and form each into a ball, using your hands. Coat each ball generously with vegetable oil and place in a lidded container. Cover and refrigerate overnight.

Shape the roti: Spread some vegetable oil on a clean work surface. Working with one ball, flatten it with the palm of your hands. Then, with your palm, press and push the dough to stretch it against the surface until paper thin, using extra oil if needed. Roll the dough in on itself to form a thin log, then roll it inward to form a scroll, tucking the end underneath. Form the remaining portions of dough.

To cook, flatten a scroll of dough to a disk 4¾ to 6 inches (12 to 15 cm) in diameter. Heat a large nonstick skillet over medium-high heat and add a little extra oil, if needed. Cook the roti on one side for 4 to 5 minutes, or until crisp and golden brown, then flip and do the same on the other side. Remove the roti canai and place it on a work surface. Fluff it up by clapping your hands from both ends to squish it in the center and help separate the layers. Keep warm on a plate, covered with a clean tea towel, while cooking the rest.

Make the butter bean curry: In a separate large skillet, heat the oil over medium heat. Add the onion, garlic and ginger, and sauté for 2 to 3 minutes. Add the curry powder, cumin, turmeric and coriander, and cook for an additional 30 seconds. Add the tomatoes and cook, stirring, until a paste is formed, about 5 minutes. Add the butter beans and vegetable stock, and simmer for 10 minutes. Stir in the coconut milk and season with salt to taste.

TAIWANESE EGG CREPE (DAN BING)

Dan bing is a culinary gem for many reasons, and if you're into Asian street food, you're going to love it. First off, it's versatile. Whether you want something simple with just egg and spring onions, or something more elaborate, such as spicy pork or shrimp, dan bing has got you covered. My version turns it up a notch by incorporating sweet corn and gooey cheese into the mixture—my personal favorite. Unlike the usual cereal or toast, dan bing offers a burst of flavors and textures that wakes you up in the most delightful way. Once you get the basics down, making it is a breeze, and it's a fun cooking project to boot.

MAKES 4 PANCAKES

----

3 tbsp (45 ml) sweet chili sauce

1½ tbsp (23 ml) light soy sauce

Rounded ½ cup (62 g) all-purpose flour

2 tbsp (16 g) cornstarch

½ tsp salt

¾ cup + 1½ tsp (182 ml) water

3 large eggs

3.5 oz (100 g) corn kernels

Rounded ½ cup (62 g) grated Cheddar cheese

2 spring onions, sliced

½ cup (120 ml) vegetable oil, divided

Make the sauce: In a small bowl, stir together the sweet chili sauce and soy sauce until well combined, then set aside.

Make the pancakes: In a medium-sized bowl, combine the flour, cornstarch and salt. Whisk in the water until a runny batter is formed. In a separate bowl, whisk the eggs and mix in the corn, cheese and spring onions.

To cook a pancake, in a large nonstick pan, heat 2 tablespoons (30 ml) of oil over medium-low heat and pour in some batter, swirling quickly until it reaches the edges of the pan. Cook until the pancake starts to set, then top with one quarter of the cheese and corn mixture. Spread it evenly across the pancake, leaving a ⅜-inch (1-cm) bare margin around the edges. Let cook until the egg mixture just sets, then flip over and cook on the other side for an additional minute. Remove from the heat and roll the pancake inward to form a log. Slice into 1½-inch (4-cm) pieces and transfer to your serving dish. Repeat to make three additional pancakes. Drizzle with the sauce to serve.

JAPANESE CABBAGE PANCAKE (OKONOMIYAKI)

Meet the ultimate Japanese street food that's about to become your new kitchen favorite! Think of *okonomiyaki* as a loaded pancake that's bursting with such ingredients as cabbage, bacon and prawns. Yep, you heard that right—cabbage takes center stage here, adding a satisfying crunch that pairs perfectly with smoky bacon and succulent prawns. It's like a party of flavors and textures in each bite! What I love most is that this dish is all about customization, so feel free to change the proteins around. Whether you're cooking for one or feeding a crowd, okonomiyaki offers a blend of simplicity and yumminess that makes it an easy win.

MAKES 2 OR 3 LARGE PANCAKES

Okonomiyaki Sauce

¼ cup + ½ tsp (52 g) ketchup

¼ cup + ½ tsp (52 g) Worcestershire sauce

2 tbsp (30 ml) oyster sauce

1½ tbsp (20 g) sugar

Okonomiyaki

1 shallot, minced

1 cup + 2 tsp (250 ml) water

3 large eggs

¾ cup + 1 tbsp (98 g) all-purpose flour

1½ tsp (12 g) salt

4 cups + 2½ tbsp (375 g) finely shredded cabbage

2 tsp (4 g) grated fresh ginger

7 oz (200 g) prawn tails, peeled and deveined, chopped roughly

4 to 6 tbsp (60 to 90 ml) vegetable oil, divided

3.5 oz (100 g) cooked thick-cut bacon, cut into 1" (2.5-cm) pieces

For Serving

Japanese mayonnaise, such as Kewpie brand

Shredded nori, for garnish

Bonito flakes, for garnish

Sliced spring onion, for garnish

Make the okonomiyaki sauce: In a small saucepan, combine the ketchup, Worcestershire sauce, oyster sauce and sugar, and heat over medium heat for 2 to 3 minutes, or until the sugar has dissolved. Remove from the heat and set aside.

Make the okonomiyaki: In a large bowl, combine the shallot, water, eggs, flour, salt, cabbage, ginger and prawn tails, and stir well. In a large nonstick skillet, heat 2 tablespoons (30 ml) of vegetable oil over medium heat, and once hot, ladle in about one-quarter of the batter. Use a spatula to shape into a large, thick round pancake. Layer several pieces of the bacon on top of the pancake. Lower the heat to medium-low and let cook until crisp and golden brown on the bottom, 8 to 10 minutes. Flip and cook on the other side until cooked through, 4 to 6 minutes.

Transfer to a serving plate and drizzle with okonomiyaki sauce, a drizzle of mayonnaise and a scattering of nori, bonito flakes and spring onion. Repeat the process for the remaining batter.

BLACK PEPPER BEEF BUNS (HU JIAO BING)

These buns, also known as *hu jiao bing*, are a staple of Taiwanese street food, featuring juicy ground beef marinated in a robust black pepper sauce all cozied up in a crispy, golden flaky bun! They have earned their street cred for a reason—they perfectly marry savory, spicy and crunchy, making them ridiculously addictive. Although they might seem a little tricky to tackle, trust me, making these at home makes them taste so much better. So, the next time you're looking to impress at a gathering, whip up a batch of these mouthwatering buns and watch your guests go wild!

MAKES 8 TO 10 BUNS

- -

Beef Filling

9 oz (250 g) ground beef

1 tsp freshly ground black pepper

1 tsp ground white pepper

½ tsp ground Sichuan pepper

1 tbsp (15 ml) light soy sauce

1 tbsp (15 ml) oyster sauce

1 tsp sugar

1 tsp sesame oil

1 tsp cornstarch

4 to 5 spring onions, chopped finely

Buns

9.5 oz (270 g) bread flour, plus more for dusting

1 tsp instant yeast

½ tsp salt

1 tbsp (13 g) sugar

1 tbsp (15 g) lard

⅔ cup + 2 tsp (170 ml) water, at room temperature

Honey glaze (1 tbsp [15 ml] honey mixed with 1 tbsp [15 ml] water)

White sesame seeds

Make the filling: In a medium-sized bowl, combine the ground beef with the black and white pepper, Sichuan pepper, light soy sauce, oyster sauce, sugar, sesame oil, cornstarch and spring onions, and stir until well mixed. Cover and let marinate, refrigerated, for 1 hour or overnight.

Make the dough: In the bowl of a stand mixer fitted with the dough hook, combine the flour, instant yeast, salt and sugar. Start the mixer on medium-low speed, and while mixing, add the lard and the warm water. Increase the speed to medium and knead until a dough is formed, 5 to 10 minutes. Remove the bowl from the stand mixer, cover with a clean tea towel and let rise in a warm place until doubled in size, about 30 minutes.

Form the buns: Divide the dough into six equal-sized portions and roll out to about 6 inches (15 cm) in diameter, using a little extra flour to dust if needed. Place 1 to 2 tablespoons (25 to 35 g) of filling in the center of a ball and pull the edges of the dough up to seal in the filling. Pinch and seal shut. Repeat with the remaining filling and dough.

To bake, preheat the oven to 400°F (200°C). Place the buns, seam side down, on a baking sheet lined with parchment paper and brush the top with the honey glaze. Sprinkle with sesame seeds and press lightly to help them stick, then bake for 20 minutes, or until cooked through and golden brown. Serve immediately.

SIX

SWEETS & BAKED GOODS

This chapter proves that life is better with a little sugar! But hold on—I'm not talking cavity-inducing sweetness here. One of the best things about Asian sweets and baked goods is how they strike that perfect balance: just sweet enough to satisfy, but not so much that you're overwhelmed. Get ready to dive into some of my personal favorites, such as Brown Sugar Bubble Tea (page 129), Japanese Soufflé Pancakes (page 133) and Hong Kong Egg Tarts (page 138).

This wouldn't be an Asian street food book without bubble tea. Think of this as your customizable, homemade bliss in a cup. The boba pearls, slow-cooked in brown sugar, give it a nuanced sweetness that you won't get from your run-of-the-mill sugary drink.

With my soufflé pancakes, you'll soar to fluffy new heights. Soft as a cloud, lightly sweet and oh so jiggly, they are the stuff of brunch dreams. Who needs regular pancakes when you can go soufflé? Oh, and you need to try my version with blueberries and cream!

And let's not forget the iconic Hong Kong egg tart—a crispy, buttery crust filled with a silky-smooth custard. This is the epitome of simple ingredients transforming into something extraordinary—especially with my kitchen hack of using store-bought pastry to cut down on time to achieve the same yummy results.

Now, why should you make these at home instead of opting for store-bought versions? Because there's something incredibly satisfying about pulling off these intricate-sounding desserts in your own kitchen. Plus, with my easy and fun recipes, you'll find that making them from scratch is totally doable and worth it. No weird additives or preservatives—just pure, homemade goodness.

THAI MANGO STICKY RICE

This classic Thai dessert is simple but so delicious. The ripe, juicy mango offers a tropical tanginess that perfectly complements the sweet, sticky rice, creating a harmonious balance that's pure magic. But wait, there's more! A sprinkle of toasted sesame seeds or mung beans (if you can source them) graces the top, adding a delightful crunch that contrasts beautifully with the creamy and chewy components of the dish. My version is finished with a drizzle of a little extra coconut sauce for that added oomph!

SERVES 4 TO 6

1 cup + 2 tsp (187 g) uncooked glutinous rice

14 oz (400 g) coconut milk

¼ cup + scant 2 tsp (57 g) sugar

½ tsp salt

Cornstarch slurry (1 tsp cornstarch mixed with 2 tbsp [30 ml] water)

3 ripe mangoes, peeled, pitted and sliced

Toasted sesame seeds, for garnish

Make the sticky rice: Rinse the rice in a fine sieve under running water until the water runs clear. Transfer the rice to a bowl, add enough water to cover, then cover with plastic wrap and let soak refrigerated overnight. Once soaked, rinse again and drain well.

Transfer the soaked rice to a heatproof bowl and set it inside a steamer basket. Steam over boiling water, over high heat, until cooked through, about 25 minutes. Once cooked, turn off the heat and set the steamer aside.

Make the sauce: In a small saucepan, combine the coconut milk, sugar and salt over medium-low heat. Stir and cook gently until the sugar has dissolved. Continue to stir over the heat while slowly pouring in the cornstarch slurry to thicken slightly. Mix half of the sauce into the sticky rice and reserve the remaining for serving.

To serve, spoon about ⅓ cup (61 g) of the coconut rice onto a serving dish. Arrange the sliced mango on the side and pour some of the reserved coconut sauce on top. Garnish with toasted sesame seeds.

CANDIED FRUIT SKEWERS (TANGHULU)

Tanghulu is a sweet, shiny snack that's as pleasing to the eyes as it is to the taste buds. A traditional Chinese treat often found at street markets, this candied fruit skewer has got a glasslike sugar coating, giving way to the juicy, tart fruit within—so it's the perfect blend of textures. This treat is not just for fruit lovers, but for anyone who appreciates a good crunch. And to top it off, it's pretty straightforward. All you need is fruit, sugar and water and with a little patience and care, you can whip up this eye-catching treat in no time!

MAKES 8 TO 10 SKEWERS

17.5 oz (500 g) mixed fruit (strawberries, grapes, mandarin, kiwi)

2 cups + 2 tsp (417 g) sugar

1 cup + 2 tsp (250 ml) water

Wash the fruit and pat it dry. Hull your strawberries; peel and separate the mandarin into sections; peel and slice the kiwi into disks. Assemble your skewers by carefully placing three to five pieces of fruit on each bamboo skewer (I use 8 to 10 skewers). You can mix up the fruit on each skewer, but I like to keep them all the same. Place on a tray and set aside.

Make the candy: In a small saucepan, combine the sugar and water. Bring to a boil over high heat and, using a candy thermometer, boil to 300°F (150°C), about 5 minutes. If you do not have a thermometer, you can test the temperature by dipping a spoon into ice-cold water, followed by into the boiling syrup. If the syrup immediately hardens on the spoon, the temperature is correct.

To finish, dip a fruit skewer into the candy syrup until well coated and transfer to a baking sheet lined with parchment paper. The syrup should harden immediately. Continue until all the skewers have been coated.

BROWN SUGAR BUBBLE TEA

This iconic bubble tea drink might look all fancy with its hypnotic swirls, but making it at home is a breeze. Believe it or not, you can whip up those chewy tapioca pearls from scratch with just a few ingredients. Plus, this classic version skips the tea entirely, making it even simpler! All you need is a blend of creamy milk and the rich, molasses-like flavors of brown sugar. Whether you're a seasoned bubble tea fan or a newcomer, this drink's effortless complexity will keep you coming back. Stir, sip, savor and enjoy!

SERVES 4

2½ cups (354 g) dark brown sugar

⅓ cup + ½ tsp (83 ml) water

3.5 oz (100 g) tapioca flour, plus more for dusting

4¼ cups (1 L) whole milk

Make the brown sugar boba pearls: In a small saucepan, combine ½ cup plus 1 teaspoon (120 g) of the brown sugar with the water over low heat. Cook gently until the sugar has dissolved. Mix in 1 tablespoon (8 g) of tapioca flour until fully incorporated, then turn off the heat and mix in the rest of the tapioca flour. Stir until a rough dough is formed, then turn out onto a work surface and knead until smooth.

Using a rolling pin, roll out to about ⅜ inch (1 cm) thick and cut into ⅜-inch (1-cm) squares. Roll into small balls, using the palm of your hands and extra tapioca starch to dust. In a medium-sized pot, bring 2 cups + 2 tablespoons (500 ml) of water to a boil and cook the brown sugar boba pearls, stirring occasionally, until cooked through, about 10 minutes. Add the remaining brown sugar and stir. Let cook for another 5 minutes.

To assemble, divide the syrup and boba equally among four tall glasses, angling the glass so the syrup catches all the sides. Add 1 cup plus 2 teaspoons (250 ml) of milk to each glass along with ice cubes and a straw to finish. Stir before drinking.

PEANUT AND TARO ICE CREAM ROLL

If you've ever roamed the bustling night markets of Taiwan, you've likely stumbled upon this unique, mouthwatering treat. At first glance, you might think, "Peanut and cilantro in ice cream, really?" But trust me, this combo works in a mysteriously delicious way. Imagine ultrathin shavings of peanut brittle enveloping a scoop of velvety ice cream, all rolled up in a delicate, crepelike wrapper. Now, add a sprinkle of fresh cilantro leaves for that surprising burst of herbal brightness. It's like a street food symphony in your mouth! Usually, this is served with peanut ice cream; my rendition takes it a step further with the use of luscious taro ice cream instead, adding a whole new layer of richness and complexity to the rolls.

SERVES 6

Taro Ice Cream

½ cup + 1 tsp (125 ml) whole milk

⅓ cup + 1 tsp (83 g) taro powder

½ cup + 1 tsp (125 ml) sweetened condensed milk

1 cup + 2 tsp (250 ml) whipping cream

Peanut Brittle

1½ tsp (15 g) unsalted butter

1¼ cups (250 g) sugar

2.5 oz (75 g) roasted peanuts, chopped

2.5 oz (75 g) roasted white sesame seeds

For Serving

6 spring roll wrappers

Fresh cilantro leaves

Make the taro ice cream: In a small saucepan, heat the milk over low heat. Once warm, whisk in the taro powder, followed by the condensed milk. Once well combined, remove from the heat and let cool. In a large bowl, beat the whipping cream until whipped and fluffy, about 5 minutes. Pour the taro mixture into the whipped cream and fold in, using a spatula, until combined. Transfer to a lidded container and leave in the freezer overnight, or until set.

Make the peanut brittle: In a medium-sized nonstick skillet, melt the butter over medium-low heat, then add the sugar. Stir until the sugar has dissolved and the mixture is boiling for about 1 minute. Pour in the peanuts and sesame seeds, and stir until well combined. Remove from the heat and pour the mixture onto a baking sheet lined with parchment paper. Let cool completely, then store in an airtight container.

To assemble, finely chop the peanut brittle or blitz it in a food processor until crumbs are formed. Place one spring roll wrapper on a flat surface and add 1 to 2 tablespoons (20 to 30 g) of the crushed peanut brittle. Add three to five cilantro leaves, then 1 to 2 scoops of the taro ice cream. Fold the two edges, the bottom edge up and over the ice cream, rolling to make a burrito. Form the remaining five rolls the same way. Serve immediately.

JAPANESE SOUFFLÉ PANCAKES

These are like fluffy, fancy cousins of regular pancakes. They're super light because they use whipped egg whites, and they're cooked in mounds to keep them tall. They take a bit longer to make, but trust me, the extra effort is worth it. Instead of stacking them and drowning them in syrup like regular pancakes, I like to serve them with lighter toppings. In my version, I serve them with a blueberry compote and fresh cream to make them extra special. So, if you're looking for a pancake that's more like a cloud, this is it!

SERVES 4

Blueberry Compote
1 lb (450 g) blueberries
Zest and juice of 1 lemon
¼ cup (50 g) sugar
Pinch of salt

Soufflé Pancakes
2 large eggs
1½ tbsp (23 ml) whole milk
¼ tsp vanilla extract
¼ cup + 2 tsp (31 g) cake flour
½ tsp baking powder
2 tbsp (25 g) sugar
Cooking oil spray
Fresh whipped cream, for serving
Fresh blueberries, for serving
Powdered sugar, for dusting

Make the blueberry compote: In a saucepan over medium heat, combine the blueberries, lemon zest and juice, sugar and salt. Cook for about 10 minutes, or until the blueberries are soft.

Make the pancakes: Separate the egg whites and egg yolks into two different medium-sized bowls. To the egg yolks, add the milk and vanilla, and whisk by hand until thick and frothy. Sift the cake flour and baking powder into that bowl, and whisk to combine thoroughly; do not overmix. Set aside while you make the meringue.

Make the meringue: Whisk the egg whites until they turn frothy and opaque. Gradually add the sugar, roughly one-third of it at a time. Then, increase the mixer speed to high and beat vigorously until stiff peaks form. It takes about 2 minutes of beating at high speed to reach stiff peaks.

Heat a large nonstick pan with a lid over low heat and spray lightly with oil spray. Add one-third of the egg whites to the egg yolk mixture, using a spatula, then gradually work in the rest. Using a small ladle, scoop some batter into the pan to make a tall mound. The pancake should consist of two to three scoops. Cook for 6 to 8 minutes, then add 1 tablespoon (15 ml) of water around the edges of the pan and cover with a lid, to steam. Cook for 2 minutes, then remove the lid and add one final scoop. Cook for an additional 6 to 8 minutes, then carefully flip and cook for an additional 4 to 5 minutes. When golden brown, transfer to a serving plate. Repeat to make the remaining three pancakes, one at a time. Top with whipped cream, blueberry compote, some fresh berries and a dusting of powdered sugar.

FILIPINO COCONUT PANDAN SAGO

This dessert is a tropical masterpiece that beautifully fuses the unique flavors found in Filipino cuisine. At the heart of this vibrant green dessert are two key ingredients: young coconut (*buko*) and pandan leaves. While coconut brings a sweet, creamy element, pandan lends a distinct, almost floral aroma, making the combination irresistibly luscious. But let's not forget about sago! These chewy tapioca pearls add not just a fun bite but also a playful look to the dessert, along with palm sugar fruit and coconut jelly. Typically served chilled, it's the perfect refreshment for hot summer days or as a palate cleanser after a hearty meal.

SERVES 6 TO 8

3 cups + 3⅓ tbsp (750 ml) fresh coconut juice

½ cup + 1 tsp (104 g) sugar

1 to 2 tsp (5 to 10 ml) pandan extract

4 tsp (12 g) agar agar powder

½ cup + 1 tsp (79 g) small tapioca pearls

1 cup + 2 tsp (250 ml) heavy cream

14 oz (400 g) sweetened condensed milk

14 oz (400 g) young coconut meat, shredded

10.5 oz (300 g) canned lychees in syrup

10.5 oz (300 g) canned coconut jelly in syrup

Make the pandan jelly: In a small saucepan, heat the coconut juice over medium heat. Add the sugar, pandan extract and agar agar powder, and bring to a boil, stirring constantly. Boil for 2 minutes, then remove from the heat and pour into a heatproof container. Set aside to cool and set, then cut into ⅜- to ¾-inch (1- to 2-cm) cubes.

Cook the tapioca pearls: In a medium-sized saucepan, bring 1 quart (1 L) of water to a boil over high heat and add the tapioca pearls. Cook, stirring every now and then, for 10 to 15 minutes, or until the pearls are translucent. Remove from the heat and drain, using a fine sieve, rinsing with cold water. Set aside.

To finish, in a large bowl, stir together the cream, condensed milk, pandan jelly cubes, tapioca pearls, young coconut meat, lychees and coconut jelly, and stir until well combined. Cover and refrigerate until chilled, then ladle into glasses to serve.

THAI BANANA ROTI

This Thai street food classic is an absolute treat for the senses! The thin, flaky dough is crisped to golden perfection, enveloping slices of ripe banana that have turned soft and gooey from the heat, finished with a generous drizzle of condensed milk that adds a layer of creamy sweetness. Now, my recipe is both delicious and simple, but you'll often find vendors adding a sprinkle of sugar or a dash of chocolate sauce, maybe even a handful of chopped nuts, to customize this to each customer's liking, so feel free to have some fun and do the same.

MAKES 10 ROTI

----

1 batch Roti Dough (page 115)

Vegetable oil

2 to 3 ripe bananas, sliced into coins

Sweetened condensed milk, for serving

Divide the roti dough into 10 equal-sized portions and form each portion into a ball, using your hands. Coat each ball generously with vegetable oil and place in a lidded container. Cover and refrigerate overnight.

Shape the roti: Spread some vegetable oil on a clean work surface. Working with one ball, flatten it with the palm of your hands. Then, with your palm, press and push against the dough to stretch it against the surface until paper thin, using extra oil if needed.

To cook the roti, heat a large nonstick pan over medium heat and add 1 tablespoon (15 ml) of vegetable oil. Carefully lift the stretched roti dough onto the hot pan. Arrange 10 to 15 banana slices in a square formation, in the middle of the roti. Fold the edges in to enclose them and make a square parcel, and let cook until crispy and golden brown, about 2 minutes. Flip and cook the other side until crisp and golden brown, another 2 minutes.

Transfer the cooked banana roti to a chopping board and cut into bite-sized pieces. Transfer to a serving dish and drizzle with condensed milk. Serve immediately.

HONG KONG EGG TARTS

These tarts can be found in bakery windows across Asia and are a real treat for the soul. First off, let's talk about texture. You've got this incredibly flaky, melt-in-your-mouth crust that pairs so perfectly with the silky-smooth custard inside. Then, there's the taste. The custard is sweet but not too sweet, with a subtle hint of vanilla. It's rich but not overpowering! So, if you're tempted to make these at home but worried about the pastry, then let me help you out with my simple kitchen hack—store-bought puff pastry. Using this not only saves you time, but it also gives you that tasty flaky crust.

MAKES 12 TARTS

- -

6 large egg yolks

½ cup (100 g) sugar

½ cup + 2 tbsp (150 ml) heavy cream

½ cup + ½ tsp (123 ml) milk

1½ tsp (7 ml) vanilla extract

2 sheets frozen puff pastry, thawed

All-purpose flour, for dusting

Canola or vegetable oil spray, for pan

Make the custard: In a small bowl, whisk together the egg yolks and sugar until light and creamy. Add the cream, milk and vanilla, then mix until well combined. Pour the custard into a pitcher and set aside.

Preheat the oven to 350°F (180°C). Shape the tarts: Stack both pieces of pastry directly on top of each other, then slice in half. Fold the stack over onto itself to form a rectangular stack of four sheets. Roll inward tightly to form a scroll, then slice into 12 rounds. Roll out each round, using a little flour to dust, then place the rounds in an oiled 12-well muffin tin. Trim any excess pastry, then pour in the custard.

Bake for 20 minutes, or until just set. Turn the setting of the oven to broil to caramelize the top of the tarts for a final 2 minutes.

BLACK SESAME BUNS

These buns are a total game changer for me. Picture a soft, pillowy steamed bun enveloping a filling that's nutty, rich and slightly sweet: black sesame paste. Originating from the world of Chinese dim sum, these buns have gone from being a hidden gem to a must-try in street food stalls and bakeries across Asia. Whether you're discovering them for the first time or you're a longtime fan, one thing's for sure: Making these buns at home can be a super fun and rewarding experience. Sure, it might take a bit of time, but the satisfaction of biting into a bun that you've made from scratch is priceless.

MAKES 10 BUNS

¾ cup + 2 tsp (113 g) toasted black sesame seeds

¼ cup (36 g) toasted peanuts

⅓ cup + 1 tsp (83 ml) melted unsalted butter

¼ cup + 1 tsp (52 g) sugar

Pinch of salt

2 tbsp (30 ml) water

1 batch Bao Bun Dough (page 42)

Make the black sesame filling: In a food processor, combine the black sesame seeds, peanuts, butter, sugar, salt and water. Process on high until a paste is formed, then transfer to a bowl. Cover with plastic wrap and refrigerate until hardened, about 1 hour. Then, using your hands, shape into 10 equal-sized balls and set aside on the tray.

To shape the buns, reknead the bao bun dough briefly, then divide into 10 equal-sized portions. Roll out each portion into a circular wrapper 4 to 4¾ inches (10 to 12 cm) in diameter, using extra bun flour for dusting, if needed. Fill with 1 heaping tablespoon (20 g) of the black sesame filling and pinch the edges around until your bun is sealed tight. Place on a piece of parchment paper. Once all the buns are formed, cover with plastic wrap to proof for 45 minutes. Then, steam gently for 10 to 12 minutes in a steamer basket over a pot of boiling water.

NOTE

- When first making the bao dough to use in this recipe, you may mix in 1 to 2 tablespoons (8 to 16 g) of crushed toasted black sesame seeds for a speckled effect and extra toasty flavor.

SOY MILK PUDDING (DOUHUA)

This isn't just any pudding; it's a smooth, creamy base of soy milk pudding that's taken to the next level with textural mung beans and the nutty aroma of roasted soybean flour. This treat has deep roots in the world of Asian desserts, and let me tell you, it's a hot item in the street food scene and very fitting for the final recipe—because it's my personal favorite. It's refreshingly light and not overly sweet, making it the perfect palate cleanser or a guilt-free indulgence. It's the kind of treat you can enjoy without a sugar overload, making each spoonful as refreshing as it is delicious. So, if you're ready to elevate your dessert game with a dish that's as versatile as it is delicious, then this pudding is your answer!

SERVES 4

Tofu Pudding

26 oz (770 ml) soy milk

2 tbsp (25 g) granulated sugar

4 teaspoons (9 g) powdered unflavored gelatin

Ginger Syrup

1 cup + 2 tsp (250 ml) water

¾ cup + 2 tsp (120 g) raw sugar

5 slices fresh ginger, julienned

Topping

Roasted soybean flour

Make the tofu pudding: In a large saucepan, combine the soy milk, granulated sugar and gelatin, and place over medium-high heat. Simmer for 5 minutes, or until the sugar and gelatin have dissolved. Do not bring to a boil. Transfer to a heatproof container, let cool, then refrigerate overnight, or until set.

Make the ginger syrup: In a small saucepan, combine the water, raw sugar and ginger, place over medium-high heat and let cook until the sugar has dissolved and the consistency thickens slightly and becomes syrupy, 15 to 20 minutes. Remove from the heat and transfer to a pitcher. Cover and refrigerate until chilled.

Assemble the tofu pudding: Ladle portions of tofu pudding into a serving bowl. Drizzle with the ginger syrup and dust with roasted soybean flour.

ACKNOWLEDGMENTS

First off, a massive shout-out to my incredible family—my Grandmère, brothers, cousins, aunties and uncles—and my rock star team at Bumplings. You've all had my back while I embarked on this cookbook journey. Your unwavering support, even if it's just keeping the Bumplings ship sailing smoothly, has been indispensable.

Mum (Dany)—You're the cornerstone of this entire project. Your daily doses of love and encouragement fuel me. Whether you're nudging me to meet deadlines or taking care of my fur baby, Tilly, while I'm engrossed in writing, your support has been monumental. Without you, this book simply wouldn't exist.

Dad (Richard)—You're a constant in my hectic life, always finding time to check in on me despite your jam-packed schedule. Let's face it, you're my street food soulmate; no one shares this culinary passion quite like you do.

Pete—More than just a father figure, you've been a guiding light in all my business ventures. Your steady support has meant the world to me. Thank you, Pete.

James—My partner in crime for epic street food adventures around the world, both in and out of the kitchen. Your support and encouragement pushes me to aim higher, and I owe a ton of this cookbook's success to you. So here it is, for the world to know: This book wouldn't be what it is without you.

Thanks, everyone—You've made this dream a reality!

ABOUT THE AUTHOR

Meet Brendan Pang, your culinary guide through the mesmerizing world of Asian street food. First capturing hearts on *MasterChef Australia* in 2018 and then 2020's *Back to Win*, he's gone on to become a culinary entrepreneur, running his own food business, Bumplings, and a line of frozen dumplings that have become a hit!

What you might not know is that Brendan's rich Mauritian heritage plays a significant role in his culinary palate. It's a beautiful blend that shines through in each dish he crafts. Already the author of two successful cookbooks—*This Is a Book About Dumplings* and *This Is a Book About Noodles*—Brendan continues to inspire home cooks with his approachable yet authentic recipes.

He was fortunate to travel around Asia growing up, soaking in the vibrant cultures and mouthwatering flavors—and he hasn't stopped: In 2023, Brendan hit the road again to seek out the tastiest street foods Asia has to offer! While writing this cookbook, he's been soaking up the creative energy of (his base) Taipei, one of Asia's street food capitals, and it's an experience that has made every recipe a true culinary gem, filled with authenticity and flair.

Brendan is more than just a home cook; he's a culinary storyteller. His recipes are narratives that intertwine traditional cooking techniques, modern twists and his unique blend of influences. Thanks to his pro tips and kitchen hacks, mastering these dishes is a breeze, no matter your cooking level. Whether you're a kitchen newbie or a cooking pro, he makes mastering these eclectic dishes simple and fun. Get ready to cook, eat and fall in love with Asian street food all over again. Happy cooking!

INDEX